TAIWAN

ENTERING THE 21ST CENTURY

The Asia Society is a nonprofit, nonpartisan public education organization dedicated to increasing American understanding of Asia and its growing importance to the United States and to world relations. Founded in 1956, the Society covers all of Asia—30 countries from Japan to Iran and from Soviet Central Asia to the South Pacific Islands. Through its programs in contemporary affairs, the fine and performing arts, and elementary and secondary education, the Society reaches audiences across the United States and works closely with colleagues in Asia.

The Contemporary Affairs Department of The Asia Society seeks to . . .

- Alert Americans to the key Asian issues of the 1980s

- Illuminate the policy choices facing decision-makers in the public and private sectors

- Strengthen the dialogue between Americans and Asians on the issues and their policy implications

The department identifies issues in consultation with a group of advisers and addresses these issues through studies and publications, national and international conferences, public programs around the United States, and corporate and media activities. Major funding for the Asian Agenda program is currently provided by the Ford Foundation, the Henry Luce Foundation, the Andrew W. Mellon Foundation, Mr. and Mrs. George O'Neill, the Rockefeller Brothers Fund, and Mr. David Rockefeller.

TAIWAN

Entering the 21st Century

by Robert G. Sutter

UNIVERSITY PRESS OF AMERICA

LANHAM • NEW YORK • LONDON

Copyright © **1988** by

University Press of America,® Inc.

4720 Boston Way
Lanham, MD 20706

3 Henrietta Street
London WC2E 8LU England

Printed in the United States of America

British Cataloging in Publication Information Available

Co-published by arrangement with
The Asia Society,
725 Park Avenue, New York, New York 10021

ISBN 0–8191–7178–6 (pbk. : alk. paper)
ISBN 0–8191–7177–8 (alk. paper)

All University Press of America books are produced on acid-free paper.
The paper used in this publication meets the minimum requirements of
American National Standard for Information Sciences—Permanence of Paper
for Printed Library Materials, ANSI Z39.48–1984.

Contents

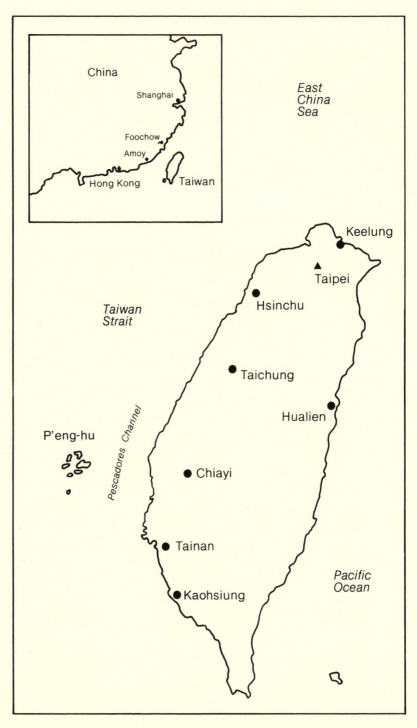

Foreword

In late 1978 the United States announced that it would no longer recognize the claim of the authorities on the island of Taiwan to be the legitimate government of all of China. Ours was not the first government to shift recognition from the "Republic of China" to the "People's Republic of China," but the announcement was nevertheless a devastating one. The United States had been Taiwan's closest friend and protector; derecognition meant withdrawal of major American troop installations on the island and removal of the Seventh Fleet from the Taiwan Strait. While few observers predicted a precipitous attack from the mainland, many worried about the long-term implications of this state of diplomatic limbo not only for the island's security, but for an economy dependent on foreign trade and a political system based on a premise that fewer and fewer nations were willing to support or accept.

Ten years later, much of that initial fear has dissipated. Taiwan has not only survived the crisis it then faced, it has flourished. Economists now describe Taiwan as one of the world's newly industrialized countries (NICs), as a "miracle" of development, and as a possible model for other developing nations. Although the number of countries that recognize the "Republic of China" hovers close to twenty, Taiwan's relations with countries like the United States, Japan, and the countries of the European Economic Community seem to be closer than ever. The New Taiwan dollar continues to appreciate against our own, and the island's foreign-currency reserves are now second only to those of Japan—and greater than those of either the United States or West Germany.

Still, there are those who remain nervous. How long can the island's economy rely on development driven by exports in an era of increasingly protectionist sentiment in the United States and other major markets? What will be the impact of extensive political reforms? What has been the social impact of economic development? And how will Taiwan survive the building pressure from the mainland authorities for increased contact and eventual reunification?

In this short monograph, Robert Sutter has tackled an extraordinarily difficult assignment: to explain how Taiwan has achieved its "miraculous" economic development and to assess these achievements in light of the challenges the island now faces. In addition to the burden imposed by space limitations, Dr. Sutter was asked not only to apply his own extensive knowledge of Taiwan, but to incorporate as well the views of sixteen other experts, all of whom participated in an Asia Society project on Taiwan. Through it all Bob Sutter has been energetic and cooperative, and I thank him for his efforts.

"Taiwan Entering the 21st Century" is a two-year outreach project of the China Council, a program of The Asia Society's Contemporary Affairs Department. The project began with a conference at The Asia Society in April 1987, at which the papers listed in Appendix A were presented. Bob Sutter served as rapporteur for the conference, with the assistance of Nancy Yang and Priscilla Armstrong. The participants were charged with identifying the key issues that became the focus of a series of public programs currently being held around the United States. The public programs, also part of the China Council project, are designed to give the American public a balanced and comprehensive understanding of Taiwan—past, present, and future. The programs began in September 1987 and will continue throughout 1988.

Many people helped to make this program possible. Major financial support for the project was provided by The China Times Cultural Foundation, whose generosity is deeply appreciated. The China Council also receives critical financial support from the Rockefeller Brothers Fund. All of the project participants have given generously of their time and ideas, often without renumeration, as have the staffs of both the Regional China Councils in Michigan, Missouri, and Oregon and The Asia Society Southern California Center, all of which have hosted programs to date: Jack Williams and Lillian Kumata in East Lansing, Joel Glassman and Katherine Pierson in St. Louis, Jane Larson in Portland, and Faranak Van Patten in Los Angeles.

As China Council director, I have received every possible form of support from Robert B. Oxnam, president of The Asia Society, and Marshall M. Bouton, director of the Contemporary Affairs Department. Linda Griffin Kean, the department's publications associate, has shepherded the manuscript from draft to final typesetting. Along the way, I have been ably assisted by Patricia Binns, Dora Ching, and Patricia Farr.

Anthony J. Kane
Director, China Council
Contemporary Affairs Department
The Asia Society
New York, NY
May 1988

This manuscript was reviewed by some of the participants in the conference on Taiwan sponsored by the China Council of The Asia Society, notably Harry Harding and Anthony J. Kane, chairman and director of the China Council, respectively. (A full list of the participants appears in Appendix B.) Richard Bush, Donald De Glopper, Beth Green, Carolyn Osborne, Andrea Savada, Roxanne Sismanidis, and Robert Worden also read and commented on the manuscript, and Nancy Shaffer and Dianne Rennack assisted in its preparation. I appreciate this assistance, but I bear sole responsbility for whatever shortcomings may be found in the study.

The views expressed in this paper are mine and not necessarily those of the Congressional Research Service, the Library of Congress, or The Asia Society.

Robert Sutter
Congressional Research Service
Library of Congress
Washington, DC
March 1988

Executive Summary

Background to the "Miracle"

During its 50 years of authoritarian colonial domination (1895–1945), Japan expended considerable effort in developing Taiwan's economy, and this became a foundation for Taiwan's later industrial development. Also under Japanese rule, a government-supported school system spread literacy, giving Taiwan an educated labor force. In 1945 Taiwan reverted to Chinese rule. Toward the end of the civil war on the mainland, as the Communists under Mao Zedong began to consolidate their victories, some two million refugees fled to Taiwan, predominantly military officials, bureaucrats, and business people. After the Communist victory, Nationalist President Chiang Kai-shek established a new and "provisional" capital in Taipei in December 1949. Just before retreating to Taiwan, Chiang Kai-shek secured a revision of the constitution granting him broad powers under a system of martial law, including the ability to restrict freedom of assembly, free expression, and political activities. President Chiang remained in office until his death in 1975, although by 1972 power had effectively been transferred to his eldest son, Chiang Ching-kuo. The younger Chiang became premier in 1972 and president in 1978, serving until his death on January 13, 1988. The organization of the ruling party, the KMT, closely parallels that of the Nationalist government at all levels, with key government and party posts often held by a single individual. Like its counterpart on the mainland, the Chinese Communist Party (CCP), the KMT is modeled on Lenin's Bolshevik Party and is responsible for determining policy.

Over the past three decades, Taiwan has changed from an agricultural to an industrialized economy. Taiwan's per capita income is estimated to be over $5,000 per year. The economy distributes wealth in a balanced way that gives all major sectors in society an important stake in continued economic progress.

Foreign trade has been a major factor in Taiwan's rapid growth over the past 30 years. The value of trade roughly tripled in each five-year period since 1955 and increased nearly four-fold between 1975 and 1980. Foreign investment, mostly from the United States, Japan, Western Europe, and Overseas Chinese in many countries, helped introduce modern technology to the island in the 1960s. Taiwan's exports have changed from predominantly agricultural commodities to 90 percent industrial goods. Imports are dominated by raw materials and capital goods, which account for more than 90 percent of all imports. Taiwan also imports more than 75 percent of its energy needs. The United States and Japan account for more than half of Taiwan's foreign trade, and the United States is Taiwan's largest trading partner. Approved U.S. private investment in Taiwan since 1954 totals over a billion dollars. Other important trade partners are Hong Kong, Kuwait, Saudi Arabia, the Federal Republic of Germany, Australia, and Indonesia. The lack of formal diplomatic relations with all but a few of its trading partners has not hindered Taiwan's rapidly increasing commerce. The maintenance of a large military establishment, which absorbs about 9 percent of the GNP and accounts for about 40 percent of the central budget, places a substantial but manageable burden on Taiwan's expanding economy. Between 1973 and 1982, GNP rose at an annual average of 9.5 percent in real terms.

The growth of Taiwan's trade in recent years has led to large trade surpluses, particularly with the United States. The resulting large foreign-exchange holdings and the inflationary pressures they have created have put added pressure on Taiwan authorities to relax controls on the outflow of capital. Initial steps in this regard were implemented in 1987.

Social Stability: A Key to Taiwan's Development

Taiwan's social stability is often credited with creating the necessary conditions for rapid economic development and with helping to avoid political disorder. While many observers admire Taiwan's social stability, others are less sanguine. They point to the role of the government's strong internal security apparatus in limiting social unrest. The tightly controlled political system, when combined with generally good economic conditions, conservative values, and traditionally strong family ties, have helped to guarantee the relative docility of the labor force, a major factor in the island's economic advancement.

Taiwan's family-centered social structure has been generally suitable for the kinds of small-scale enterprises that have been the backbone of the island's economic success up to the present. But the tightly knit family structure in Taiwan may prove to be incompatible with the broader-scale economic enterprises Taiwan is said to need to remain competitive in the international economic environment. If so, the result could be a decline in prosperity, which in turn could cause social and political tensions that may undermine the island's stability.

Nationalist government officials have attempted to use policy to provide opportunity for economic and social advancement, and there is a direct relationship between the Nationalist government's economic policies and the rise of new middle-class groups. Through the promotion and expansion of the public and private sectors, the state development strategies have pushed the small landowners into the ranks of the urban industrial workers class or the middle classes, which have emerged as the mainstay of this newly industrialized capitalist society. By 1980 only 18 percent of the island's employed population engaged in farming activities, and of them, over 90 percent were actually part-time farmers. At the same time, the emerging working and middle classes have become more visible in their social and political impact. The key lesson of these changes for the people of Taiwan is that the majority of the middle classes, old and new, have come from lower-class groups and have benefited from the upward social mobility seen in the postwar period. However, the rise of the middle classes gives rise to growing expectations. If class structures were to solidify as a result of less rapid economic growth or other changes, this could generate frustration and anxiety for both the middle classes and those below them.

Taiwan's Role in the World Economy

Economic modernization lies behind many of the important social and political changes seen in Taiwan in recent years. This rapid economic transformation reflects complex relationships among economic growth, income distribution, and productivity. Another crucial factor in the solution of economic problems over the past 30 years has been the effectiveness of the government's role; government policies have fostered innovation, nurtured flexibility in the economy, and provided encouragement and incentive.

These administrative efforts can be classified into three categories. First, the government pursued policies to restructure economic incentives, particularly by the redistribution of property rights. Second, government policies shifted resources from low to high value-added products by inducing more competition, channeling the flow of economic activity in new ways, and facilitating the role of markets. Finally, the government inaugurated policies to achieve equilibrium within the economic system by offsetting certain kinds of scarcities. The government remains strongly committed to using its power to facilitate economic growth through these types of policies. The state continually intervenes in the market through new legislation and policies aimed at providing stable growth and ensuring that the gap in income distribution between rich and poor sectors of society does not widen as growth takes place. The state also strives to minimize unemployment and maintain stable price levels.

Some economic experts caution that the newly industrializing countries (NICs) of East Asia (Hong Kong, Singapore, South Korea, and Taiwan) may not be able to maintain their rapid export growth rates of the recent past, and that, therefore, because of their high foreign-trade dependency, their overall economic growth rates may begin to decline. Singapore's negative or low growth in the mid-1980s is cited as a case in point, and its difficulties are said to have broader implications for similar, export-oriented countries in the region, including Taiwan. Taiwan's physical resources are limited. The island's economy is heavily dependent upon foreign trade for the raw and finished materials with which to produce goods and services for domestic use and foreign sale and for its supply of energy. Exports constitute around 55 percent of GNP, which makes the current trend of international protectionism particularly worrisome and adds some validity to the arguments of those who see a gloomy future for Taiwan and other NICs.

Over the long run, Taiwan seeks to maintain high growth rates and high productivity, keep unemployment and inflation low, and protect its balanced income distribution. Many factors make Taiwan's prospects for achieving these goals favorable. Taiwan's business firms and households have great resiliency, are frugal, strive to be efficient and highly productive, and—perhaps most important—remain ready to respond and adapt to new market forces. It is this flexibility that should enable the economy to continue to outperform most other economies in coming decades. Given continued social and political stability and peaceful conditions along the Taiwan Strait, Taiwan should be able to upgrade productivity in its manufacturing and service sectors; continue to have high savings and make the necessary investment in new capital to improve economic performance and product quality; and maintain markets in foreign countries by which to earn the foreign exchange needed to purchase the necessary raw materials and products from abroad.

To achieve these goals, Taiwan will have to meet and overcome a number of international and domestic economic pressures. For example, increased international protectionism threatens Taiwan's export base, and Taiwan's trading partners continue to pressure for an opening of its market, appreciation of the New Taiwan dollar, and other structural reforms. Taiwan also faces the domestic challenges of an aging population and the need to develop indigenous science and technology capabilities.

The Evolving Political System

While Taiwan's social stability and economic development are widely admired, its political system is much more controversial. Debate centers on the degree of "authoritarianism" in the one-party Nationalist rule. During 1987 the Nationalists, under President Chiang Ching-kuo, began a process of reform that involved ending the 38-year martial law regime, considering an overhaul of parliamentary bodies brought over from mainland China in the 1940s, and allowing the political opposition to organize and form a viable opposition party. The incentive to change has come from several sources. Most important of these were the rising demands of opposition politicians—backed by elements of the middle class and workers—for increased opportunity to participate in the political life of Taiwan. Another factor has been the problem of leadership succession posed by the passing of President Chiang.

On July 14, 1987, President Chiang Ching-kuo ended martial law and agreed to lift a ban on opposition parties after 40 years of authoritarian rule. Although rival political parties remained illegal until the revision of statutes governing "civic organizations" was completed, the ruling Nationalist Party (KMT) took no steps to dismantle the island's main opposition party, the Democratic Progressive Party (DPP).

The DPP was formed from a loose coalition of non–KMT legislators and political activists known as the *tang-wai* ("party outsiders"). Prompted in part by the success of democratic movements in South Korea and the Philippines, *tang-wai* activists formally established the DPP in September 1986. Despite pressure from right-wing groups and conservative elements within the KMT, Chiang Ching-kuo took no formal repressive action against the DPP. In December 1986 DPP candidates campaigned in legislative elections and doubled their representation in the country's highest parliamentary organs. However, the DPP has displayed internal generational and ideological divisions, and opinion is divided over whether the DPP will hold together or will split into a number of competing parties.

The majority of DPP members share these common goals: complete renewal of membership to the assemblies through elections; release of political prisoners; freedom of the press, freedom to establish new political parties, and freedom of assembly and demonstration; accelerated admission of native Taiwanese to positions of political power; popular election of the governor of Taiwan province and the mayors of Taipei and Kaohsiung, who are now appointed by the central government; repeal of the National Security Law; and divestment of KMT business interests. The DPP groups its agenda for legislative reform under the umbrella term of "self-determination." For moderate members of the DPP, self-determination means greater political power for the majority Taiwanese. Other members of the DPP assert—at least implicitly— that the Taiwanese electorate would abandon the goal of reunification if given a choice. In this view, self-determination could be seen as a veiled call for Taiwan independence.

Pressures for reform became more urgent in recent years in light of the impending death of President Chiang Ching-kuo. Upon Chiang's death in January 1988, Vice President Lee Teng-hui, a native of Taiwan and a Cornell-trained agronomist, took over as head of state and acting chairman of the KMT. He will serve out the remainder of Chiang's term, which ends in 1990. Lee Huan, who was appointed secretary-general of the Kuomintang in July 1987, is another key figure in the new administration. He is a long-time supporter of a process whereby native Taiwanese have been promoted to positions in government formerly held by mainlanders. Nevertheless, the reformers run up against the more conservative inclinations of many older numbers of the KMT's Standing Committee, and there is also said to be opposition to rapid reform on the part of leading military and national security figures. It is still unclear how far the KMT wants to take reform and whether or not recent liberalization will survive the loss of Chiang's leadership.

Several major factors will determine whether President Lee Teng-hui will be able to maintain political stability or whether the leadership transition will be interrupted. Perhaps most important will be the attitude of the majority of people on Taiwan concerning the limits on their political rights under the present system. From one perspective, their demands for political participation have increased less than many outside observers expected. And while there have been some demands for expanded political participation, on the whole the Nationalist leadership has proven remarkably adept at adjusting political institutions to absorb and/or selectively to repress these demands.

xvi

Political tensions on Taiwan may also be held in check by Taiwan's international political and economic environment and by its Chinese sociocultural heritage. Taiwan's domestic political development is constrained by its position in global geopolitics and the global economy, both of which seem to require some democracy but not too much. Any radical redefinition of domestic political legitimacy could entail an equally radical redefinition of Taiwan's international political status. In particular, a wholesale abandonment of Taipei's claim to be the legitimate government of China and the establishment of a formally separate status for the island probably would not be supported by Taiwan's friends abroad and could provoke intervention by the People's Republic.

Economically, any appearance of domestic political instability could affect the flow of trade, investment, and technology on which Taiwan's domestic prosperity depends. On the other hand, many foreign businessmen believe that gradually increased political participation for the population on Taiwan is more likely to produce a disciplined work force and stable investment climate than will heavy-handed repression. Taiwan's Chinese sociocultural heritage also is seen to strongly condition both the extent of pressure for political change and the interplay among political elites. Taiwan's formal political institutions are relatively recent imports from abroad, grafted onto traditional Chinese values of deference to age, cultivation of networks, and preference for mediation over confrontation.

Taiwan's political system is likely to become more liberalized and democratic. What may be needed now is a set of new rules and fresh formulas for reallocating political power and public resources to meet the opposition's rising expectations without causing severe damage to the vested interests of the beneficiaries of the current system. In short, the task will involve complicated compromise among contending political forces. Looking toward the 21st century, one sees at least three broad political issues that may shape the future evolution of Taiwan's political system: institutional changes involving the ruling Nationalist Party's relationships with both the state and society; political succession and composition of political leadership; and legitimacy of Taipei as the government of China.

Taiwan's International Role

Taiwan suffered a series of major diplomatic setbacks in the 1970s which culminated in the breaking of relations with the United

States in 1979. Only about twenty nations now recognize the Taipei government. Among them, only South Korea, Saudi Arabia, South Africa, and the Holy See possess significant international status. Yet Taiwan's international status has improved modestly in the 1980s, and specialists point to a combination of several factors to explain this improvement: the actions of and balance of power among the major countries in Asia, the politics and policies of the PRC, and Taiwan's growing global economic stature.

During the 1980s the balance of power in Asia seemed to shift in a direction more favorable to the United States, Japan, and their friends, including Taiwan. A more cautious Soviet policy is aimed more at accommodating regional interests than at seeking advantage through serious disruption of the prevalent balance of influence. This policy change seems to have enhanced regional stability and assisted those Asian states, including Taiwan, that appeared to have little to gain from forceful change in the regional geopolitical status quo.

The concurrent preoccupation of the People's Republic of China with internal development also appears to have reduced the likelihood of provocative PRC policy toward the island. The primary concerns of PRC leaders have been to guarantee Chinese national security, maintain internal order, and pursue economic development. Especially since the death of Mao Zedong in 1976, the priority of top leaders has been to promote successful economic modernization, which they see as the linchpin of their success or failure, and they have geared China's foreign policy to help the modernization effort. Nationalistic and ideological objectives regarding issues like Taiwan have generally been given secondary priority. Thus, as part of its effort to build international support for its modernization program, Beijing has sought to expand ties with the United States, Japan, and other neighboring non-Communist countries, while playing down differences with them. For many, this so-called independent foreign policy of peace has indeed contributed to peace throughout the region.

Perhaps of most importance to Taiwan, the United States has appeared more confident and powerful in Asia in recent years—a contrast with the decade of U.S. withdrawal from the region during the 1970s following the Vietnam War. Increased U.S. confidence vis-à-vis the Soviet Union has been translated into a relative decline in past U.S. interest in using military and other relations with the PRC as a major source of strategic leverage—a "China card" in global competition with the Soviet Union. Although U.S.–PRC military ties have continued to develop, they and other

xviii

Sino-American relations have progressed at a gradual and deliberate pace that has not alarmed other American friends in the region, including Taiwan.

Despite its favorable international environment, however, Taiwan is directly affected by changes in policy on the mainland. During recent years, the PRC has not ceased to put pressure on Taiwan to establish ties and eventually to reunify with the mainland. And the PRC leadership has been aware of the subtle linkage between the Hong Kong issue and the Taiwan issue; that is, a heavy-handed approach toward one will inevitably damage the prospects for successfully handling the other. Furthermore, news of Taiwan's economic success has spread further and deeper into the Chinese mainland, making a policy based on threats of force more difficult to justify on PRC national interest grounds. In short, Beijing has found little advantage in a hard-line policy in the absence of a direct provocation from Taiwan. Quite conscious of the possibility of change in PRC policy and the international environment, Taiwan officials have taken care not to provoke the PRC directly, nor to upset the evolving U.S.–PRC relationship.

A third major determinant of Taiwan's international role is its increased economic might. Taiwan has used its growing profile as a major international economic actor to work quietly to strengthen bilateral ties with the United States and with many Asian countries.

Despite such favorable trends, however, analysts remain sharply divided over whether Taiwan will continue to survive and develop as a viable international actor. In all likelihood, the power relations in Asia during the next decade, particularly Sino-Soviet relations, will be different and more complex than they have been in the recent past. One should not be too surprised if some or all of the "three obstacles" now claimed by Beijing to be existing in Sino-Soviet relations—Chinese opposition to the Soviet military buildup along China's northern border, Soviet support for Vietnam's occupation of Cambodia, and the Soviet military occupation of Afghanistan—were to be removed one by one in the next fifteen years.

While Moscow will neither abandon its acquired security interests in Asia nor pass up any opportunity to advance its interests at the expense of the United States, the Soviet Union is likely to translate its new-found interest in Asia into concrete policies. Under Mikhail Gorbachev, the Asia-Pacific countries, often neglected by Soviet diplomacy in the past, will get much more attention. To the extent possible, Moscow will seek to supplement its military power with other policy instruments.

A number of developments may complicate Washington's future role in the region. The recently more assertive U.S. trade policy may clash increasingly with the development needs of the Asian countries. At a minimum, bilateral trade issues will continue to vex U.S.–Taiwan relations for the foreseeable future. Domestic troubles in two of Washington's key allies in the region, the Philippines and South Korea, will create painful dilemmas for U.S. policy as both countries struggle to make progress toward democratization. The United States may also face uncertainties growing out of the complexities of a possible Sino-Soviet rapprochement and internal PRC politics. Under these circumstances, some judge that it is not inconceivable that a new U.S. administration would move to accommodate the PRC's demands at the expense of Taiwan, for fear of setting back important U.S.–PRC strategic, economic, or political relations.

As for the impact of the PRC's policy on Taiwan, several things are clear. First, the PRC will not likely abandon its desire for reunification. Second, if political trends in Taiwan and the mainland were to diverge further, this could create more pressure for Beijing to pursue an active policy toward Taiwan: pressing for greater contacts, trade, and interchange and working with third parties (e.g., the United States) to push Taiwan to be more open to PRC gestures. Since Taiwan's economic and, perhaps to some extent, political relations with other countries are likely to grow as its economy expands, Beijing may also attempt to tighten its pressure on Taiwan by isolating it diplomatically, particularly in Asia.

Perhaps of more importance will be Taiwan's handling of the situation in Hong Kong as the colony reverts to PRC control. The absorption of Hong Kong into the PRC under the rubric of "one country, two systems" means that after 1997 Taiwan must regard Hong Kong as part of the PRC. If Taiwan were to apply to Hong Kong the policies currently applied to the PRC, a wide range of relationships between Taiwan and Hong Kong would come to an end. Continuing to treat Hong Kong as an entity distinct from the PRC would have important advantages for Taiwan. The question is how such treatment could be rationalized and how its possible adverse effects on Taiwan's policy toward the PRC could be minimized.

In sum, the interests of the regional powers are not served by substantial disruption of the status quo. And the Taiwan leaders have sufficient prudence to avoid actions (such as declaring independence) that would seriously undermine the regional status quo that has proven, on the whole, favorable to Taiwan's peace and prosperity.

I. Introduction

In 1949 Chiang Kai-shek fled the Chinese mainland and established an exile government on the island of Taiwan. In June 1950, with the outbreak of war in Korea, the United States sent its Seventh Fleet into the Taiwan Strait, and for 28 years the U.S. government continued to recognize the Nationalist government's claim to be the sole government of China. Although relations were severed when the United States recognized the People's Republic of China on January 1, 1979, commercial and cultural ties between the United States and Taiwan have continued to be close.

American relations with Taiwan are complicated by the continued claim by both Beijing and Taipei to be the legitimate government of China. Neither will allow the United States or any other country to maintain diplomatic relations with both. And while military tensions in the Taiwan Strait have subsided as U.S.–PRC relations improve and Beijing focuses on a policy of peaceful reconciliation with Taiwan, PRC leaders have refused to renounce formally the right to use force, if necessary, to settle the "Taiwan issue." The issue therefore remains a central one in Sino-American relations and occasionally in domestic U.S. politics as well.

Taiwan's economic success has also become an increasing cause of tension in relations with the United States. A rapidly growing U.S. trade deficit with the island has led to protectionist sentiment and, most recently, the removal of Taiwan and the other Asian "tigers" (Hong Kong, Singapore, and South Korea) from the General System of Preferences.[1] Taiwan has responded with a combination of policies which seek at once to open further its own markets and to lobby against protectionism in the U.S. Congress.

Domestic political strife in Taiwan has also drawn attention in the United States, especially following the suspicious death in 1982 of a Carnegie Mellon University professor (a Taiwanese national), who died while visiting Taiwan, and the 1984 murder of Henry Liu, a U.S. citizen who wrote an unauthorized biography of Taiwan President Chiang Ching-kuo, in a suburb of San Francisco. Combined with an increasingly vocal opposition movement in Taiwan and among Taiwanese-Americans in the United States, these

---

[1] The General System of Preferences (GSP) was established in 1976 to provide temporary tariff incentives to help developing countries enter the U.S. market and diversify their manufactured exports. Duty-free status was granted to some 3,000 products from 141 countries.

1

events have focused attention on issues concerning human rights and political liberty on the island that claims to represent "free" China. The recent lifting of martial law and other liberalizations have begun to blunt this kind of criticism.

The loss of diplomatic relations with the United States is only one aspect of Taiwan's difficult international position. The People's Republic of China replaced Taiwan at the United Nations in 1971. Since then, Taiwan's diplomatic position has been gradually eroded as more and more countries have changed their official recognition from Taipei to Beijing. Currently, Taiwan has formal diplomatic ties with only about twenty countries, most of them in Latin America.

Given this often dramatic and controversial history of Taiwan-related developments during the past four decades, it is not surprising that for many Americans Taiwan is increasingly seen as a "problem" in Sino-American relations, U.S. human rights policy and in U.S. economic relations with the Asia-Pacific region. In effect, public affairs groups, media commentators, political leaders, and many scholars have tended to view Taiwan from a wholly external perspective. Little attention has been paid to the process by which Taiwan achieved its economic "miracle" while handling problems created by its ambiguous international status.

In this monograph Taiwan is treated differently. Rather than examining Taiwan solely from the vantage point of American concerns, this study assesses Taiwan from the inside out. That is, this study is an attempt to assess as comprehensively as possible, within the confines of this brief book, domestic developments in Taiwan's economy, society, culture, and politics; to examine their effects on the future stability, prosperity, and international standing of Taiwan; and, in the end, to review Taiwan's position in international affairs and in U.S. foreign policy in particular. Such an approach is important, first, because Taiwan has undergone a remarkable internal and international transformation in recent years and is likely to continue to change well into the 21st century, and, second, because American interests in Taiwan are increasingly determined by these economic, social, and political changes. The Taiwan authorities' ability to deal with tensions created by their own aggressive trade policies and with the social consequences of aspirations created by the growing wealth of a largely native Taiwanese middle class could have at least as important an impact as traditional strategic concerns, both domestically and in Taiwan's relations with the United States and other countries around the world.

An understanding of Taiwan's society and culture is crucial for an overall understanding of the people on the island today and of their rapid economic development in recent decades. This includes an understanding of the strong family system and the role of literature, art, and historical tradition in defining cultural trends and identity, and the role of U.S. political and economic support in promoting a sense of well-being and social stability. While Taiwan's evolution from a traditional, rural society to a modern, urban one is typical of developing nations, it reflects an unusual mix of influences. Taiwan's culture and society are basically Chinese, but native Taiwanese and mainland Chinese roots have been infused with the influence of a half-century of Japanese colonial rule (1895–1945) and a strong postwar relationship with the United States. The resulting social structure and culture are unique, and some would argue that it has been this unique mixture of influences that has produced the Taiwan "miracle." The people on Taiwan generally have enjoyed a rapidly rising material standard of living, most notably a rise in the education level of the general population and an ever-increasing percentage of people attending colleges, universities, and technical schools.

While such economic prosperity generally has fostered urbanization and a newly wealthy middle class, in Taiwan economic growth has been accompanied by an impressively narrow gap between the incomes of rich and poor. Cleavages among people with different incomes have remained relatively small. Once-serious social divisions between the 15 percent of the population who came from the Chinese mainland with the Nationalist forces in the late 1940s ("mainlanders") and the 85 percent of the population whose roots on the island pre-date the late 1940s ("Taiwanese") continue to diminish. Taiwan's new president, Lee Teng-hui, is the first native Taiwanese to serve in that post. Several factors underlie Taiwan's social stability, including the growth of economic opportunity and continuing strong family ties that provide a firm social foundation. Section II of this book offers a brief background to Taiwan's development, reviewing the island's history and outlining its current political, economic, and social system. Section III will review the unique social and cultural factors that have greatly shaped Taiwan's rapid economic growth.

The Taiwanese show strong tendencies to save and to work hard, and they have been ingenious in adapting and improving their products in response to the demands of the international marketplace—all key factors in remaining internationally competitive. While some observers are therefore optimistic about Taiwan's economic future, others are less so. Pessimists point out that underneath the current social stability lies a widespread feeling of anxiety

3

and doubt about Taiwan's identity and about a future that could have a negative impact on economic development in a highly competitive international environment. Others worry about the impact of persistent PRC efforts to promote reunification with the Communist mainland. Moreover, there is concern that some of the features of Taiwan's current social stability (e.g., close family ties) impede the formation of broad economic enterprises that Taiwan may need in order to remain internationally competitive. Can Taiwan maintain its comparative advantage in a competitive international economic environment? Is the island's present financial, regulatory, and corporate structure adequate to meet the needs of the next stage of development? How will the authorities deal with growing displeasure in the U.S. Congress over Taiwan's steadily increasing trade surplus and foreign-currency reserves? Section IV outlines Taiwan's recent economic modernization, reviews the government's development strategies, and assesses the outlook for continued growth of the island's economy.

Economic and social change lies behind the growing trend toward political liberalization of the Nationalists' authoritarian, one-party rule. In particular, in 1987, President Chiang Ching-kuo announced the end of the 38-year-old regime of martial law, substituting a new National Security Law. For the first time, an opposition party has been allowed to organize and run candidates in elections; and the Nationalist government has begun to take what promise to be unprecedented steps to reform the parliamentary institutions in order to give the people of the island greater say in managing their own political affairs. The next few years will be a crucial transitional period.

Economic prosperity, higher levels of education, and other changes bring higher expectations on many fronts, and an increasingly sophisticated populace has intensified pressure for reform. There are growing demands for a less arbitrary and more representative political system that will be responsive to popular demands for change over a range of questions involving environmental protection, working conditions, and transportation. How has the political structure of the Nationalist government evolved, and what does this tell us about the likely future course of political reform? Will President Lee Teng-hui be successful in building a new leadership coalition in the post-Chiang era that can maintain the island's remarkable record of social and political stability? Can the newly organized political opposition party be effective, and will a legitimate two-party system emerge? What are the ramifications of the self-determination issue raised by opposition leaders? In partic-

4

ular, will such developments prompt the People's Republic to become more assertive in its efforts to pressure Taiwan into reunification talks? Section V will discuss Taiwan's evolving political system and the challenges facing efforts at further reform.

Taiwan's ambiguous role in international affairs is familiar to many Americans. Taiwan is not recognized as the legal government of China, or even as a national entity, by the vast majority of its trading partners, including the United States and Japan. Taiwan's international standing, future domestic policy, economic development, and its informal web of international ties with the United States and other countries are directly affected by international economic issues such as Taiwan's large trade surplus with the United States and domestic political issues such as political reform and liberalization. Beyond these concerns are issues focused on the Taipei government's attempts to secure arms and advanced technology, its efforts to resist PRC pressures toward reunification on the "one country, two systems" model, and more broadly, Taiwan's ability to define its relationship with the rival regime in Beijing. The book will conclude with a review of Taiwan's present and future international standing.

II. Background to the "Miracle"

Chinese migration to Taiwan is thought to have begun as early as A.D. 500, and passing references to the island were made by Song dynasty historians in the tenth century.[2] However, the first major influx of migrants from the Chinese mainland did not come until the seventeenth century, sparked by political and economic chaos on the China coast during the twilight of the Ming dynasty. A European presence was established in Taiwan in 1624, when Dutch traders claimed the island as a base for commerce with Japan and the China coast. Dutch colonists administered the island and its predominantly aboriginal population until 1661.

In 1661 a Chinese fleet led by the Ming loyalist Zheng Chenggong (known in the West as "Koxinga") retreated from the mainland and occupied Taiwan. Zheng expelled the Dutch and established Taiwan as a base in his attempt to restore the Ming dynasty. Zheng died shortly thereafter, and in 1683 his successors submitted to Manchu control.

The Manchus, who established the Qing (Ch'ing) Dynasty (1644-1911), ruled Taiwan as a frontier district until it was declared a separate Chinese province in 1886. During the eighteenth and nineteenth centuries, migration from China's coastal provinces of Fujian and Guangdong steadily increased, and the Chinese supplanted the aborigines as the dominant population group. In 1895 a weakened imperial China ceded Taiwan to Japan following the first Sino-Japanese war.

During its 50 years of authoritarian colonial domination (1895-1945), Japan expended considerable effort in developing Taiwan's economy. The Japanese established agricultural research stations, farmers' cooperatives, and large-scale irrigation projects that transformed Taiwan's agricultural economy into a thriving market economy. The construction of a modern transportation network and a series of hydroelectric and thermal power plants was the beginning of an economic infrastructure that became a foundation for Taiwan's later industrial development. Also under Japanese rule, a

---

[2] Basic sources of background information on Taiwan include U.S. Department of State, *Background Notes: Taiwan* (September 1985); Congressional Research Service, *Taiwan: Recent Developments and their Implications for the United States*, Issue Brief No. 87092 (updated monthly); U.S. Department of Commerce, *Foreign Economic Trends, Taiwan* (updated annually); U.S. Congress, House, Committee on Foreign Affairs, *Country Reports on Human Rights Practices for 1986* (Washington, DC: U.S. Government Printing Office, 1987).

government-supported school system spread literacy, giving Taiwan an educated labor force.

In 1945 Taiwan reverted to Chinese rule. The Chinese Nationalist authorities from the Chinese mainland were repressive and corrupt, which led to extreme Taiwanese discontent. Anti-mainlander violence flared on February 28, 1947. The uprising was swiftly and brutally suppressed by Nationalist troops, with an estimated 10,000 people killed, including many key leaders of the Taiwanese community. The incident left a legacy of distrust between Taiwanese and mainland Chinese.

Toward the end of the civil war on the mainland, as the Communists under Mao Zedong began to consolidate their victories, some two million refugees fled to Taiwan, predominantly military officials, bureaucrats, and business people. After the Communist victory, Nationalist President Chiang Kai-shek established a new and "provisional" capital in Taipei in December 1949.

Taiwan's Political Evolution

Just before retreating to Taiwan, Chiang Kai-shek secured a revision of the constitution granting him broad powers under a system of martial law. These powers, enforced by the military's Garrison Command, included the ability to restrict freedom of assembly, free expression, and political activities. President Chiang remained in office until his death in 1975, although by 1972 power had effectively been transferred to his eldest son, Chiang Ching-kuo. Chiang Kai-shek's vice-president, Yen Chia-kan, succeeded to the presidency upon Chiang's death but never truly ruled. The younger Chiang became premier in 1972 and president in 1978, serving until his death on January 13, 1988.

Both Chiangs served concurrently as head of the government and as chairman of the ruling party, the Kuomintang (KMT). The organization of the KMT closely parallels that of the Nationalist government at all levels, with key government and party posts often held by a single individual. Like its counterpart on the mainland, the Chinese Communist Party (CCP), the KMT is modeled on Lenin's Bolshevik Party and is responsible for determining policy. The government's job is to carry out that policy.

Beneath the President's Office, the government is composed of five administrative branches, or Yuan: Executive, Legislative, Control, Judicial, and Examination. Two are elected bodies, and the remaining three are appointed by the president. All are dominated by the ruling party. The two elected bodies, the Legislative Yuan and the Control Yuan, are controlled by mainlanders who were elected for life before the government moved to Taiwan. However, an attrition due to death and a gradual expansion of the total number of available seats have led to a gradual increase in the proportion of Taiwanese-born members in these two bodies and in a third elected body, the National Assembly.

Under the 1947 Chinese constitution, to which the Nationalists still adhere, the "sovereignty of the people" is exercised by the National Assembly, a body formed through elections held that year throughout China. Seated in Taipei, the Assembly presently has about 990 serving members. The National Assembly elects the president and vice-president (in practice, it has approved the KMT's choices), and it has the power to amend the constitution. It also has the as-yet-unexercised powers of initiative and referendum.

The main lawmaking body is the Legislative Yuan (Parliament), which originally had 773 seats under the 1947 constitution. To reflect Taiwan's growing population, the authorities ordered supplementary elections to add 11 new members in 1969, when they also added new members to the National Assembly. In 1972 triennial elections were inaugurated to fill the supplementary seats. In 1980 an additional 97 new seats were added. However, with the death or incapacitation of many older legislators elected in 1947–48, many seats from mainland districts remain unfilled, and the Legislative Yuan now has about 250 serving members. Mainlanders elected before 1949 are still in the majority, although the percentage of younger parliamentarians elected on Taiwan is growing.

With the consent of the Legislative Yuan, the president appoints the "premier" of the Executive Yuan, which constitutes the Cabinet and has primary responsibility for policy execution and administration. The other members of the Cabinet (i.e., Executive Yuan) are appointed by the president on the recommendation of the premier. The premier is in overall charge of the Executive Yuan and supervises the operations of its ministries and other subordinate agencies.

The Control Yuan is composed of members elected by provincial and municipal councils and includes representatives of Mongolia, Tibet, and Chinese residing abroad. It monitors the efficiency of the civil service and investigates instances of corruption. Before 1980 the Control Yuan consisted of 42 members of the original 180 elected in 1948 and 10 supplemental members elected for six-year terms beginning in 1972. In 1980 the number of elective Control Yuan seats was increased by 22, and another 10 seats were created

8

for appointees from among Overseas Chinese communities elsewhere in Asia.

The Judicial Yuan includes the seventeen-member Council of Grand Justices, which like the U.S. Supreme Court, interprets the constitution. The Council's jurisdiction includes civil, criminal, and administrative cases and cases concerning disciplinary measures against public functionaries. All members of the council, as well as the president and vice-president of the Judicial Yuan, are appointed by the president. The subordinate organizations of the Judicial Yuan are the Supreme Court, the High Courts, the District Courts, the Administrative Court, and the Committee on the Discipline of Public Functionaries.

The Examination Yuan functions as a civil-service commission. It comprises two ministries: the Department of Examination, responsible for recruiting public functionaries through competitive examination, and the Department of Personnel, in charge of the registration of public functionaries, transfers, promotions, and commendations.

Below the central government is the Taiwan Provincial government, located in central Taiwan at Chunghsing New Village, near Taichung. The central government exerts control over the provincial government in several ways. In particular, the governor of Taiwan Province and the mayors of Taipei and Kaohsiung are appointed by the central authorities. The Provincial Assembly, the key legislative body of the Provincial government, and local city councils are elected by popular vote and have some limited authority over local affairs.

Until recently, this tightly controlled political system left little room for the expression of opposition views. Two minor political parties, the Democratic Socialist Party and the Young China Party, were permitted to exist but had no significant influence or following. After the Legislative Yuan elections in December 1980, however, a group of non–KMT legislators known as the tang-wai (literally, "party outsiders") began to coalesce into effective informal caucuses that, through skilled management of parliamentary procedure, gave the non–KMT politicians a measure of influence in central policymaking. Together with moderate Nationalist Party legislators, the tang-wai became a political force with the potential to change representative politics in Taiwan.

In September 1986, opposition politicians, in defiance of the still-existent ban on the establishment of new political parties, announced the formation of the Democratic Progressive Party (DPP). Though the DPP was technically illegal, the government authorities took no action against it and did not interfere with the convening of its first Party Congress in November 1986. DPP candidates campaigned under their new party's banner in elections held in December 1986 and won over 20 percent of the vote. Composed of competing political factions held together by common opposition to the KMT, the DPP remained active in 1987 and was expected to be formally legalized once the government amended statutes governing political organizations.

What has led to these recent changes in the political system? Many observers point to the creation of a new middle class made financially independent and politically bold by Taiwan's economic success. These factors will be explained more fully below, but much of the credit must go to Chiang Ching-kuo, who first as premier and then as president proved more sensitive than his father to the pluralistic nature of the island's population. While he sought to maintain the effectiveness of the KMT and state apparatus and to protect the positions of the mainlanders who dominate them, Chiang also sought to open up the political process to allow more Taiwanese participation. In July 1987 martial law was lifted in favor of a new National Security Law. The new law still allows the government to employ security measures when desired.[3] Furthermore, opposition to basic policy (such as expressing views contrary to the authorities' claim to represent all China or supporting an independent legal status for Taiwan) is still considered seditious. In other ways, however, personal and press freedoms have been expanded.

Although friction between mainlanders and native Taiwanese on the issue of native enfranchisement remains a problem, it has abated with time and the gradual melding of the two communities. In 1972 Chiang Ching-kuo (then premier) began a concerted effort to bring Taiwanese into more senior positions in the central administrative apparatus. Taiwanese now hold almost half the ministerial positions in the Cabinet and over a third of the positions on the KMT's leading body, the Central Committee. Of some two million KMT members, about 70 percent are Taiwanese. Taiwanese hold most of the elective and appointive positions at the provincial and local levels. President Lee Teng-hui, whom Chiang chose as his vice-president, is a Taiwanese and succeeded as head of the government and acting chairman of the party.

---

[3] For example, hours after Chiang Ching-kuo's death, President Lee Teng-hui declared a 30-day ban on street demonstrations and rallies and placed the police and military on full alert. *Far Eastern Economic Review* 139:4 (January 29, 1988), p. 19.

Economic Development

Chiang Kai-shek brought from the mainland a relatively sophisticated bureaucracy, party organization, and military establishment much larger than what was required to rule Taiwan. Despite the burden this bureaucracy has placed on the island's limited resources, it contributed to the authorities' ability to implement policies that, aided by generous U.S. aid in the early years and sustained by the hard work of the local population, greatly facilitated the island's rapid modernization. Over the past three decades, Taiwan has changed from an agricultural to an industrialized economy. Taiwan's per capita income is estimated to be over $5,000 per year. The economy distributes wealth in a balanced way that gives all major sectors in society an important stake in continued economic progress. The benefits of economic prosperity have tended to offset the political costs of opposition to the 40 years of authoritarian, one-party rule by the Chinese Nationalists.

Foreign trade has been a major factor in Taiwan's rapid growth over the past 30 years. The value of trade roughly tripled in each five-year period since 1955 and increased nearly four-fold between 1975 and 1980. Foreign investment, mostly from the United States, Japan, Western Europe, and Overseas Chinese in many countries, helped introduce modern technology to the island in the 1960s. Taiwan's exports have changed from predominantly agricultural commodities to 90 percent industrial goods. Imports are dominated by raw materials and capital goods, which account for more than 90 percent of all imports. Taiwan also imports more than 75 percent of its energy needs. The United States and Japan account for more than half of Taiwan's foreign trade, and the United States is Taiwan's largest trading partner. Approved U.S. private investment in Taiwan since 1954 totals over a billion dollars. Other important trade partners are Hong Kong, Kuwait, Saudi Arabia, the Federal Republic of Germany, Australia, and Indonesia. The lack of formal diplomatic relations with all but a few of its trading partners has not hindered Taiwan's rapidly increasing commerce.

After years of focusing on production of "light industry" consumer goods for export, efforts are being made to develop more sophisticated heavy industry and technology-intensive industry. Taiwan's economic future is based on a shift in industrial structure toward one that is more capital intensive and more energy efficient. Taiwan's economic policymakers aim for export industries to account for 80 percent of the gross national product (GNP) by 1989. They also have indicated that they hope to reduce Taiwan's reliance on U.S. and Japanese markets and to compete with U.S. and Japanese manufacturers, while becoming a major trading partner with South America and Africa. Their plans forecast the industrial sector of GNP will increase 10 percent annually, while agriculture's share will continue to decline.

Between 1973 and 1982, GNP rose at an annual average of 9.5 percent in real terms. During the recession following the 1973 oil-price shocks, Taiwan managed to overcome the slump in demand for its industrial exports by adopting a successful economic stabilization program. Also, ten major infrastructure projects were launched to stimulate economic activity. Taiwan's economic planners hoped that the sharp increase in investment for the major projects, coupled with revived demand for the island's exports, would establish the basis for continued prosperity. While not all the projects were seen as successful, recent performance generally confirms that earlier optimistic forecast.

Most of Taiwan's ten major infrastructure projects were completed by the end of 1978. They included a north-south freeway linking the major cities of western Taiwan; a new international airport at Taoyuan near Taipei; railway electrification, modernization of the island's ports, and construction of a new port near Taichung; a rail link from Suao to Hualien; the island's first integrated steel mill; a major shipyard at Kaohsiung; petrochemical plants; and additional electric power plants.

In late 1977 twelve new projects were announced, most of them complementary to the original ten projects. These included construction of additional highways, completion of a rail network around the island, completion of the second phase of the integrated steel mill, construction of the island's second and third nuclear power plants, expansion of Taichung harbor, construction of new towns and housing, improvement of irrigation and flood control, financing for farm mechanization, and construction of local cultural centers. The projects were designed to ensure progress in transportation and electric power, an improved industrial base, and accelerated farm modernization. The major construction period, 1979–84, was aimed at bringing Taiwan into the ranks of the developed economies by 1989—a goal that seems within reach.

About 30 percent of the cost of these projects has been financed through foreign capital. The authorities encourage foreign investment to help finance the island's efforts to move away from light, labor-intensive, export-oriented industry to more capital-intensive production for export and for secondary import substitution. The electronics industry is the most important industrial export sector and is the largest recipient of U.S. investment. Textile production, although of declining importance, remains Taiwan's second most important industrial sector. Other important export industries include plastics, toys, sporting goods, footwear, and furniture. Taiwan's industrial structure is highly labor intensive, taking advantage of the island's skilled and moderately salaried labor force.

Much of Taiwan's industrial production takes place in export-processing zones (EPZs) such as those in the Kaohsiung Harbor area, at Nantze near Kaohsiung, and at Taichung. EPZs combine the advantages of an industrial zone and a free-trade area and have attracted considerable foreign investment. But a great deal of production for export also takes place in small factories located throughout the island that are linked by Taiwan's efficient transportation system. In addition, improved port and harbor facilities in Taiwan have been keeping up with sharply rising demand, and international air-transport service is excellent. Kaohsiung is the world's fourth-largest container port.

The maintenance of a large military establishment, which absorbs about 9 percent of the GNP and accounts for about 40 percent of the central budget, places a substantial but manageable burden on Taiwan's expanding economy. The armed forces number about 500,000. Two-thirds are ground forces, and the rest are split about evenly between air and naval personnel, including marines. The reserves total more than two million troops. Conscription is universal for men over age nineteen. Taiwan's armed forces are equipped with weapons obtained primarily from the United States, but in recent years, stress on military "self-reliance" has resulted in the growth of domestic military production in certain fields. Taipei adheres to the nuclear Non-Proliferation Treaty and has stated repeatedly that it does not intend to produce nuclear weapons.

The growth of Taiwan's trade in recent years has led to large trade surpluses, particularly with the United States. The resulting large foreign-exchange holdings and the inflationary pressures they have created have put added pressure on Taiwan authorities to relax controls on the outflow of capital. Initial steps in this regard were implemented in 1987.

Taiwan's agricultural sector is extremely productive. Although only about one-quarter of the island is arable, virtually all farmland is intensively cultivated, with some areas suitable for two and even three crops per year. Increases in agricultural production have been much slower than in the rapidly expanding industrial sectors.

Although self-sufficient in rice production, Taiwan imports large amounts of other food grains, mostly from the United States. Meat production and consumption are rising sharply, reflecting a rising standard of living. Taiwan exports large amounts of frozen pork. Other agricultural exports include sugar, canned mushrooms, canned asparagus, bananas, pineapples, citrus fruits, fresh vegetables, and tea. Taiwan has a large fishing fleet and is an important exporter of fish. Deep-sea as well as offshore fisheries have grown steadily each year. While government planners and entrepreneurs will probably devote considerable attention to the agricultural sector in the future, it seems clear from recent trends that more rapid growth and development is to be found in industrial and higher-technology products.

The United States, Taiwan, and the People's Republic of China

Reflecting the special relationship established between the United States and the Chinese Nationalist government of Chiang Kai-shek during the Second World War, Americans watched with great attention and concern the Nationalists' retreat to Taiwan in 1949. After the start of the Korean War in June 1950, America was again defending and providing aid to Chiang's Nationalists, who were seen by many as providing a strategic asset, an "unsinkable aircraft carrier" in the chain of defenses the United States was building to contain the spread of communism in Asia. A well-publicized debate between General Douglas MacArthur and the Truman administration regarding the possible utility of Chiang's forces in the war against the Chinese Communists in Korea was an important factor behind President Harry Truman's eventual dismissal of MacArthur.

The potential for military conflict between Chinese Communist and Chinese Nationalist forces in the Taiwan Strait during the 1950s set the context for American debate over the extent of the U.S. defense commitment to Chiang's Nationalists. Congressional ratification in 1955 of the U.S. security treaty with the Nationalist government was accompanied by the passage of the "Formosa Resolution," which attempted to define carefully the limits of the U.S. commitment to defend Quemoy and Matsu, the small islands near the mainland coast that were still held by the Nationalists. The seriousness with which Americans viewed the fate of the islands was reflected in a debate between John F. Kennedy and Richard Nixon in 1960, the first major televised debate in a U.S. presidential campaign. Considerable time was taken in debating just how far the United States should go in defending the islands.

14

U.S. frustration with the protracted conflict in Vietnam during the late 1960s prompted the Nixon administration to reassess the twenty-year-old U.S. policy of containment. The Sino-Soviet split in the 1960s, President Nixon's opening to Beijing in 1972, and the major pullback of U.S. forces in Asia in the late 1960s and early 1970s changed the American view of the mainland government. Relations with Beijing were now seen more as a strategic asset in the U.S. struggle against the Soviet Union. Americans redefined their interests in Taiwan accordingly. The issue was no longer how the United States could work with Chiang's Nationalists to block the expansion of the common enemy, Communist China. Instead, the issue became—and remains—how to find a proper balance between improving relations with the People's Republic of China on the mainland, a strategically important new friend, and maintaining good relations with the Nationalists on Taiwan.

The issue crystalized in 1979 when the Carter administration broke official ties with Taiwan as a precondition for establishing diplomatic relations with the PRC. This prompted another serious policy debate over the continued U.S. commitment to Taiwan. The debate culminated in the passage in early 1979 of the Taiwan Relations Act (TRA), Public Law 96–8, to govern the ostensibly unofficial U.S. ties with Taiwan. Congress extensively amended the draft law submitted by the Carter administration in order to strengthen language underlining the continued U.S. interest in the stability, economic prosperity, and security of the people on Taiwan. In particular, the act promised continued U.S. shipments of military equipment for Taiwan's defense against possible military action by the mainland.

Debate over how to strike a proper balance in U.S. relations with Taiwan and the PRC also figured prominently in the 1980 presidential race, with candidate Ronald Reagan calling for a restoration of official U.S. ties with Taiwan. After he took office, however, President Reagan gradually came to endorse the past policy of attempting to improve relations with the strategically important mainland while maintaining close, albeit unofficial, ties with Taiwan.

American commercial and cultural interaction with the people of Taiwan is facilitated through the American Institute in Taiwan (AIT), a nongovernmental entity. The institute has its headquarters in Washington, D.C., and field offices in Taipei and Kaohsiung. Staffed largely by U.S. State Department and other officials who are temporarily "separated" from the U.S. government, AIT is authorized to accept visa and passport applications and to provide assistance to U.S. citizens in Taiwan. A counterpart organization, the

15

Coordination Council for North American Affairs (CCNAA), has been created by Taiwan. It has headquarters in Taipei and field offices in Washington, D.C., and ten other U.S. cities.

On January 1, 1979, at the time of derecognition, the United States notified the Taiwan authorities of its intent to terminate the 1954 Mutual Defense Treaty. That termination took effect January 1, 1980, but the United States in its unilateral statement released on December 16, 1978 (issued concurrently with the joint U.S.–PRC communiqué establishing bilateral relations), declared that it "continues to have an interest in the peaceful resolution of the Taiwan issue and expects that the Taiwan issue will be settled peacefully by the Chinese themselves."

Since derecognition, the United States, in accord with the TRA, has continued the sale of selected defensive military equipment and defense technology to Taiwan. This has prompted often strong objections from the PRC. U.S.–PRC negotiations in 1981 and 1982 led to the August 17, 1982 U.S.–PRC joint communiqué addressing this point. In that communiqué, the PRC cited a "fundamental policy" of striving for a peaceful solution to the Taiwan question. With that Chinese policy in mind, the United States stated in the communiqué that "it does not seek to carry out a long-term policy of arms sales to Taiwan, that its arms sales to Taiwan will not exceed, either in qualitative or quantitative terms, the level of those supplied in recent years since the establishment of diplomatic relations between the United States and China, and that it intends to reduce gradually its sales of arms to Taiwan . . . ."

Future arms sales to Taiwan are to accord with the policies contained in the August 17, 1982 communiqué. In conjunction with the issuance of that communiqué, President Reagan issued a statement that

> regarding future U.S. arms sales to Taiwan, our policy, set forth clearly in the communiqué, is fully consistent with the Taiwan Relations Act. Arms sales will continue in accordance with the act and with the full expectation that the approach of the Chinese Government to the resolution of the Taiwan issue will continue to be peaceful . . . . The position of the U.S. Government has always been clear and consistent in this regard. The Taiwan question is a matter for the Chinese people, on both sides of the Taiwan Straits, to resolve. We will not interfere in this matter or prejudice the free choice of, or put pressure on, the people of Taiwan in this matter. At the same time, we have an abiding interest and concern that any resolution be peaceful.[4]

[4] Cited in U.S. Department of State, Bureau of Public Affairs, *Background Notes: Taiwan* (September 1985), p. 8.

16

U.S. commercial ties with Taiwan have been maintained and expanded since derecognition. Taiwan continues to enjoy Export-Import Bank financing, Overseas Private Investment Corporation guarantees, most-favored-nation status, and ready access to U.S. markets. The U.S. Agency for International Development's Mission in Taiwan closed, however, in 1965, long before derecognition. More than $1.7 billion in U.S. economic aid was provided between 1949 and 1965.

The switch in U.S. recognition and the 1982 communiqué on arms sales to Taiwan did not remove the so-called Taiwan issue in U.S.–PRC relations. Specifically, for many years Beijing has encouraged Taipei leaders to begin talks leading to a peaceful reunification of Taiwan with the mainland. PRC leaders find that continued U.S. support, especially U.S. arms sales, reduces Taipei's interest in negotiations. Beijing thus concludes that smooth U.S.–PRC relations will require the removal of what it sees as the continued "obstacle" of U.S. arms sales to Taiwan.

It is against the backdrop of events described above that Taiwan has emerged as the economic power and international anomaly that it is today. The rest of this monograph will look more closely at Taiwan's present society, economy, domestic polity, and international status in order to better understand where the island might be headed on the eve of the 21st century.

III. Social Stability:
A Key to Taiwan's Development

Taiwan's social stability is often credited with creating the necessary conditions for rapid economic development and with helping to avoid political disorder. Stability and growth have been conducive to both foreign and indigenous investment. Although there is a residue of uneasiness between mainlanders and Taiwanese, the passing of time seems to be reducing its importance. And, significantly, class differences (e.g., between the middle and working classes) that have emerged with economic modernization have not been as important in Taiwan as in other rapidly developing countries. In particular, Taiwan's development has been characterized by comparatively narrow gaps between the income levels of rich and poor groups and by a low level of potentially disruptive class consciousness.

While many observers admire Taiwan's social stability, others are less sanguine. They point to the role of the government's strong internal security apparatus in limiting social unrest by restricting potentially disruptive gatherings, curbing labor unions, restricting strikes, and penetrating, through informers and covert or overt government agents, other potentially disruptive organizations. These practices, when combined with generally good economic conditions, conservative values, and traditionally strong family ties, have helped to guarantee the relative docility of the labor force, a major factor in the island's economic advancement. However, these critics observe that Taiwan's newly prosperous middle class and its intellectuals often feel alienated from the current order and anxious about the future. These groups' search for clearer identity, purpose, and dignity could challenge the political status quo in ways detrimental to continued stability.

There are a whole range of additional questions regarding the suitability of Taiwan's social structure for future economic change. Taiwan's family-centered social structure was generally suitable for the kinds of small-scale enterprises that have been the backbone of the island's economic success up to the present. But the tightly knit family structure in Taiwan may prove to be incompatible with the broader-scale economic enterprises Taiwan is said to need to remain competitive in the international economic environment. If so, the result could be a decline in prosperity, which in turn could

18

cause social and political tensions that may undermine the island's stability.

The Family-Centered Economy

In many ways, the structure of the Taiwanese economy is a product of the values that govern the behavior of the family, which constitutes the basic unit of production. While export-oriented industry may appear to foreigners to be the most prominent sector of the Taiwanese economy, this sector neither employs the broadest segment of the Taiwanese labor force nor reflects the broader economic goals of the Taiwanese people.

Factory Work Since the industrial boom of the later 1960s, about one-fifth of Taiwan's labor force has worked in large industrial enterprises. Physically easier than farming and other forms of more menial labor, factory work also pays better, is performed indoors, and still has the attraction of being more "modern" than other forms of labor. Jobs in big, export-oriented factories are mostly taken by men and women in their teens. About half of all factory workers are between the ages of fifteen and twenty-four. Young women make up one-third of this important workforce.

Large factories actively recruit young workers from the countryside, providing them with inexpensive, barracks-like housing, canteens, limited medical services, and some recreational activities. Workers for smaller factories often live with relatives or in cheap apartments rented in the poorer neighborhoods and suburbs. While some young people appear to enjoy the opportunity to leave home and escape parental restraint on their daily activities, others become homesick or disillusioned with the dull work routines, the limited opportunities for advancement, and unpleasant experiences with dishonesty, exploitation, and insincerity that are often encountered in an urban environment. Young women especially complain that these factors add up to a new understanding that life "out in society" is unpleasantly "complicated" (fuza), or corrupt. Also, the relatively higher wages earned by young factory workers do not result in much economic freedom. Many parents of unmarried factory workers expect their children to remit home almost all their wages for family capital accumulation or to pay family expenses, including school fees for their brothers. Sons are less likely to comply with these demands, but daughters often feel they have no choice. In fact, while wages are relatively higher than in other sectors, factory wages remain low; US$25 per month was a common wage in the late 1960s, and in 1987 it had reached only about $300.

The dangers of factory life are not only social, they also can be physical. Some work, such as assembling microchips, is widely believed to result in rapid deterioration of eyesight, and many other factory workers are exposed to unguarded machinery and toxic substances. A worker in an asbestos-weaving factory told one observer:

> Your whole body gets covered with asbestos fluff. . . . There is no air-conditioning, and in the summer you are sweaty and sticky over your whole body. The company says they can't put in air-conditioning because the fiber is too damp and the air-conditioners would get clogged . . .[5]

Asbestos, of course, causes both asbestosis and cancer.

The desire for better working conditions, better wages, and expanded worker rights that such experiences engender has been held firmly in check by strict laws against labor organizing and strikes. These measures had been given added weight by martial law until its repeal in July 1987. Another factor dampening labor unrest is the short-term nature of most factory workers' employment. Factory work is rarely a life-long occupation. Factories generally discourage the employment of married women, a pattern reinforced by the custom of bearing children soon after marriage. Men withdraw from factory employment as they mature because factory wages are rarely adequate for a growing family and because the discipline and routines become increasingly hard to bear. They try to find other kinds of work, very often as small, independent businessmen. As women round out their families and consider returning to income-producing work, they too look for opportunities outside the factory system. Many start small shops or restaurants, work part-time as servants or service personnel, or finish products at home for larger industries.

These "retirees" are soon replaced by another generation of cheap, docile youths who will work for little more than it takes to support one person. In recessions, they are easily laid off, for many can return to work in their families' farms and small businesses. This pattern of movement in and out of factory work has been a great advantage to factory owners, Chinese and foreign. This cheap and flexible labor supply does not bargain, strike, bring political

---

[5] Cited in the paper presented by Hill Gates to The Asia Society Conference on Taiwan, April 1987, entitled "Working Class Taiwan."

pressure to bear, or even settle down in working-class neighbor-hoods near the factories.

Household Businesses As the goals and opportunities of the family play a key role in determining the nature of factory work, so do they affect the economic and social behavior of another key social group, the many petty capitalists who aspire to middle-class status. To become the owner of a family business is a nearly universal goal within the working class in Taiwan. It is hard to exaggerate just how small these enterprises can be. An old story tells of a rich man who began his career by buying five peanuts for a single small coin and selling them for two. There are still many businesses that start with a minimum of capital. The sellers of "shoulder pole noodles," well known in Tainan City, carry an entire restaurant—stove, cookpot, ingredients, dishes, and a stool for the customer—in two boxes slung on a shoulder pole, from which they produce bowls of delicious noodles. In the late evening the streets of all Taiwan's cities swarm with slightly larger versions of these portable restaurants, usually mounted on bicycle-powered carts. For a small fee, they plug into an electrical outlet in a nearby house, turn on the bulb, and set up shop for evening strollers.

Many small businesses are more substantial: rice-milling shops, tailoring establishments, barber shops and beauty parlors, grocery stores, photography studios, and a multitude of small factories that produce everything from bean curd and incense sticks to electronic sub-assemblies for bigger factories. Increasing demand for traditional handicraft products has expanded trade for many craftspeople who supply domestic and foreign markets with such goods as Chinese medicines and fine furniture.

Petty capitalists participate in the market not as individuals, but as families. The decisions of individuals depend not only on immediate opportunity and capacity, but also on the needs and abilities of the entire family. Decisions about family labor reach into the choices young people make about marriage partners and the number of children they will have. The wishes of family seniors still have much weight in these matters. Many small businesses use the labor of the family alone or add the help of a young relative or friend's child as an apprentice, although the more successful employ wage workers as well. Most small businesses maximize security and minimize overhead by occupying a part of the family house and are attended to by household members in between other activities such as housework and child care, school attendance and homework, watching television and entertaining vistors, or selling

21

products. People in such businesses work extremely hard, but they also have the kind of control over their own actions that factory organization was designed to prevent. This is often cited as the reason for the popularity of small businesses.

Family members do not receive wages but draw on family funds when they need money. These funds are managed by the wife or mother-in-law, who may also regularly distribute a little pocket money for cigarettes, snacks, or movies. Family members work at jobs for which their talents and other commitments suit them, not for the short-run reward of wages but for the long-term good of the family. If jobs are plentiful "outside" and pay better than the value a family member can contribute at home, the family urges that person to look for work and mobilizes its network of contacts to help find it. When a family member working "outside" is laid off, she or he returns home and is reabsorbed into the family economic unit.

In 1986 enterprises with fewer than ten workers made up nearly 70 percent of all businesses. Such small businesses are rational and positive adaptations to Taiwan's economy because they use labor in a flexible and inexpensive way—workers put in long, hard hours, sometimes in return for only simple shelter, food, and clothing. In prospering households the family workers will receive a more comfortable standard of living and luxuries: some can pursue higher education, daughters may enter marriage with dowries, and some may receive shares in a growing investment of capital in the house and business. Through education, some young people in economically stable families escape the necessity of manual labor or shopkeeping by finding white-collar jobs as office workers for the government or large private businesses, but very few people can achieve such education by their own efforts.

Working-class families often have several members who work, ideally in a variety of occupations. A shop for the mother or her daughter-in-law to manage, a family construction firm for the husband and oldest son, a job as a clerk in a bank for the better-educated younger son, and a factory place for an unmarried daughter make a nice mix: stability, though low income, from shop and clerking; bigger wages, if intermittently, from skilled housebuilding; and a little extra cash from the daughter's paycheck. Many parents deliberately steer offspring into such combinations and readily shift work to seize new opportunities.

Petty-capitalist households are supported in their economic endeavors by highly developed "informal" institutions: day-to-day business is facilitated by personal moneylenders, rotating credit associations, or word-of-mouth recommendations; ritual occasions, such as temple festivals and family ceremonies, indicate income levels and the ability to raise large sums and thus serve to attract clients; and substantial, predictable capital transfers occur at marriage and family division. Neighborhoods, temple parishes, and kin networks heavily supplement and sometimes completely replace formal financial institutions; highly personalistic ties cement business partnerships even among the largest private businesses.

Government Policy, Economic Development, and the Rise of the Middle Class

Many observers say Taiwan's social stability and economic advancement owe much to the dedication and vision of Nationalist government officials who have attempted to use policy to provide opportunity for economic and social advancement. Indeed, one can draw a direct relationship between the Nationalist government's economic policies, which have led to Taiwan's rapid development, and the rise of new middle-class groups.

Beginning in early 1949, and with a greater push in the early 1950s, the Nationalist authorities started implementing a far-reaching and highly successful land-reform program. The redistribution of land among small farmers had a number of beneficial social, political, and economic effects and led to a significant increase in farm production. In the land-reform program, the Nationalist authorities compensated large landowners with commodities certificates and stock in state-owned light industries. Although some landowners were left impoverished by the compensation, others were able to turn theirs into capital with which to start new, nonagricultural commercial and industrial enterprises. These new entrepreneurs became Taiwan's first industrial capitalists, who, with refugee businessmen from the mainland, managed Taiwan's transition to a more commercial, industrial economy.

After the completion of land reform, the Nationalist state started its first four-year economic plan, from 1953 to 1956, advancing "import substitution industrialization" (ISI). This development strategy was continued through the Second Four-Year Plan (1956–60) and was aimed at creating an indigenous industrial sector for products needed in the domestic market to displace imported consumer goods. Nevertheless, although the state facilitated a protectionist trade policy and despite the fact that domestic industrial and entrepreneurial capabilities grew during this time, the state

23

was reluctant to move to foster and create a genuine private sector in Taiwan due to political and practical considerations. The ideological emphasis on state enterprises, as advocated by Nationalist Party founder Sun Yat-sen, was still influential among government officials. And the Nationalists, predominantly mainlanders at the time, did not completely trust the local Taiwanese entrepreneurs. Furthermore, the very limited capacity of the private sector in postwar Taiwan did not seem to be an attractive and viable target for the state's attention. Thus, the state-owned enterprises and the mainlander-owned private industries were the leading beneficiaries of the ISI strategy. A first generation of local Taiwanese industrialists also emerged, of which the largest group was landlords-turned-capitalists.

Another by-product of the ISI strategy was the creation of the first generation of urban industrial workers in both state and private industries. As a group, small farmers began to decline, and the self-employed and the unpaid family workers also began to drop in number. White-collar workers in the private sector increased, joining already considerable numbers of white-collar workers in the government bureaucracy and state enterprises. In sum, the growth of the ISI private industries, the expansion of the state enterprises, and growth of the state administrative bureaucracy provided an environment in which a predominantly Taiwanese middle class was slowly emerging between the dominant mainlanders and the rapidly growing Taiwanese working class.

In the early 1960s the Nationalist state shifted its economic strategy to a new approach emphasizing "export-oriented industrialization." Beginning as a trial-and-error effort without any definite and clear expectations, this approach stressed developing manufacturing industries aimed at promoting exports into the world markets, particularly the United States. Starting from the Third Four-Year Plan (1962–64) and lasting effectively to the end of the Fifth Plan (1969–72), the private sector rapidly expanded, leading to a large increase in the number of local entrepreneurs. Small and medium-size enterprises grew, existing side by side with larger, more well-established industries controlled by mainlanders and Taiwanese. The number of urban industrial workers, concentrated in the private sector, also grew faster than before, and a more viable and energetic group of Taiwanese entrepreneurs and professionals emerged. These trends saw the rise of the new middle class in the modern industrial and commercial sectors. The expansion of state bureaucracy of both central and local levels also gave rise to middle-class, white-collar workers in the state sector.

From one perspective, the state-guided development strategies in the past three decades have radically transformed Taiwan's post--land reform social structure. Through the promotion and expansion of the public and private sectors, the state development strategies have forcefully and successfully pushed the small landowners into the ranks of the urban industrial workers class or the middle classes, which have emerged as the mainstay of this newly industrialized capitalist society. By 1980 only 18 percent of the island's employed population engaged in farming activities, and of them over 90 percent were actually part-time farmers. It is clear that as a group, the small farmers, without any political power coalition and with little other bargaining power, have lost most of their influence. At the same time, the emerging working and middle classes have become more visible in their social and political impact. In the past three decades the workers as a group increased from less than 15 percent to more than 40 percent of the total population, while the middle classes rose from about 20 percent to more than 30 percent. Within the middle classes, the ranks of the new middle class (managers and professionals) have increased, while the size of the old middle class (small shop and property owners) has been stable. In the 1980s the new middle class and the old middle class consisted of about 20 percent and 10 percent respectively, a ratio of 2:1.

The key lesson of these changes for the people of Taiwan is that the majority of the middle classes, old and new, have come from lower-class groups and have benefited from the upward social mobility seen in the postwar period. They serve as an example of the potential for upward social and economic mobility, and as such, they reinforce stability. However, there are potentially negative consequences of these changes. In particular, the rise of the middle classes gives rise to growing expectations. If class structures were to solidify as a result of less rapid economic growth or other changes, this could generate frustration and anxiety for both the middle classes and those below them.

Prospects for Continued Social Stability

Why haven't such frustrations and anxieties developed and led to greater social cleavage along class lines? And why have the working and middle classes remained so remarkably stable throughout this period of unprecedented change? The broad scope for economic opportunity and advancement in Taiwan provides one explanation. Another lies in the role of the extended family as a means of breaking down barriers between key social groups, notably petty capitalists, who are or aspire to be part of the middle class, and the part-time proletariat. Others suggest that Taiwan's family-centered social structure may not be as conducive to economic growth and political stability in the future as it has been up to now. Still others characterize Taiwan as a society in ferment below the surface, especially within the more well-to-do middle class and among the intellectuals, who are seen to be striving for new identity and culture amid a mix of sometimes conflicting values. We will examine each of these views in turn.

The Extended Family as a Stabilizing Force Industrial workers and household entrepreneurs are the over-producers on whom Taiwan's economy clearly depends. It might easily be assumed that these categories of people constitute two quite separate groups, each tending to produce its own class culture that is passed on to children who enter occupations similar to those of their parents. But this is not the case. Although there are dirty and discouraging industrial cities like Sancheng and Kaohsiung where a factory culture is emerging, a very large proportion of workers in large corporations, especially the multinationals, are only part-time members of the proletariat. As noted earlier, factories hire them in their late teens and early twenties for a few years—two or three in electronics assembly, up to ten in other industries. Then, in large numbers, they "retire" to take up other occupations. The majority of Taiwan's industrial workers are raised in rural and urban petty-capitalist households and return to or found such households as soon as they can after "selling their green years" to corporate employers. Thus, the apparent distinctions between small entrepreneur and factory worker is an illusion.

A vehicle that serves to break down these and other potentially disruptive class distinctions is the extended family. It lies at the center of personal networks for urban and rural residents, binding them to one another and to kin in other parts of Taiwan and abroad, destroying in the process the neat social distinction between urban and rural, middle class and lower class, domestic and foreign. These kinds of family-centered personal networks provide much of the social cement that supports stability and economic development on Taiwan.

What is the nature of these families, and how do they work? The family, or *jia*, is a group of people related by blood, marriage, or adoption, whose defining feature is the joint ownership of property

26

by males in the group.[6] Within the family, authority relations are hierarchically arranged, with power and authority relatively centralized in the senior generation. Within this group, relations between generations are guided by a set of widely agreed upon and culturally stressed obligations, according to which parents have the duty to help provide for their children's education, jobs, spouses, and, for sons, shares of the family property. In return for this, children are duty bound to contribute to the family economy, and sons have the additional obligation of supporting their parents in their old age. Despite Taiwan's advanced level of modernization, these norms are still widely followed. Parents now have fewer children but give them more education, find them better jobs and spouses, and give them more property when the family divides.

While families everywhere go through cycles of growth and dissolution, in the Taiwan family, cycles can be very complex and are very important determinants of other things. Practically all aspects of family organization change as the family passes through its developmental cycle, i.e., as it gains more members and generations. Though some families last for decades, in time all families divide. In general, up until the time of family division, the further along a family is in its development, the greater its ability to use traditional mobility strategies (described below) and the greater its income, wealth, and social status. Because property is divided equally among sons, the more wealth a family amasses before division, the greater the decimation that occurs at family partition. Vast industrial empires—often headquartered in Taipei but dispersed all over East and Southeast Asia—are regularly broken up by family division. Thus the family is a property-holding unit and must be sharply distinguished from the household, a co-residential unit. Since families may contain any number of households, households are often simply fragments of families rather than bounded socioeconomic units. Households can be sorted into "primary households," which contain the family's economic manager and redistributor, who are usually one and the same person, and "secondary households," which contain other people, often members of the younger generation.

Each family tends to be a relatively self-contained unit, with each individuals' loyalty riveted to the family. This family-cellular nature of Taiwan's society and economy is both a strength and a weak-

[6] For a more detailed discussion of the significance of the *jia* and many of the other issues discussed in this section, see Susan Greenlaugh, "Networks and Their Nodes: Urban Society on Taiwan," *The China Quarterly* 99 (September 1984), pp. 529–52.

ness. It is a strength because Taiwan's families are driven by an intense desire to improve their fortunes. In striving to move up the ladder of success, families on Taiwan employ a number of strategies that promote not only their own mobility but also the socioeconomic development of the society as a whole. Among these strategies are family extension, advanced education, short-term migration (sojourning), economic diversification, and property accumulation.

Yet the economic success achieved through these strategies has not been without cost. For example, because the family is an inward-looking unit whose members reserve their deepest trust for each other, there is a strong preference among people on Taiwan, as among Chinese generally, for economic relationships based on prior acquaintance and trust. When one must go outside the family circle to find a creditor, worker, or the like, one goes first to the next concentric circle—those with whom one has some prior social relationship—and then to the surrounding circle—those with whom an acquaintance has a prior relationship. This highly personalistic structure of economic relationships has important consequences for the labor market. First, it means that an impersonal labor market in which workers are selected on universalistic criteria alone is minimally developed. At least 70 to 75 percent of the migrants to Taiwan's cities find jobs through relatives and friends. Workers hired without personal introductions feel no compunction to stay when their friends leave, when their families need their help at home, or if they can earn better wages elsewhere. Others stay until they learn the ropes, then leave and set up their own firms, which then become competitors of the original firm. While this pattern is tolerated by Taiwanese employers—many of whom did the same thing themselves—it is not appreciated by foreign employers, who have become wary of hiring local managers and technicians.

Another cost stems from the highly atomistic, competitive nature of Taiwan's society. Each unit acts first and foremost to advance its own individual interests. In doing so, it often competes with other families—who are pursuing their individual interests—in ways that are mutually detrimental or destructive. Family atomism lies behind the "swarm of bees" phenomenon about which entrepreneurs constantly complain yet to which they regularly contribute. The swarm of bees occurs when one family enters a lucrative line of business, dozens of others leap in, prices are forced down, and the profits for everybody fall.

Family Loyalties as a Brake on Development Few would disagree that on balance the family system has shaped the island's urban and economic development and its linkages with other parts of the world or that it has reinforced social stability in Taiwan. Simply by pursuing its own social mobility, the family has facilitated Taiwan's high levels of education, urbanization, economic diversification, and industrial dispersion. By providing its own "social security," the family has increased the resources available to the government for solving larger developmental problems, particularly as the population ages. Through its patterns of dispersal, extension, and finally division, the family has mitigated inequalities between urban and rural areas, ethnic groups, and social classes. By exploiting kinship and community networks, family firms have produced the low-cost goods and services that have spurred Taiwan's entry into the select ranks of newly industrialized countries. And by dispersing members abroad, families have created transnational networks that provide social links between Taiwan and countries to which it is not linked politically or diplomatically.

While family-based economic activity served Taiwan well in the labor-intensive stage of its development, some observers, including some policymakers in Taiwan, are worried that it may offer a less efficient basis for development in the current capital- and technology-intensive stage. They see Taiwan's future prosperity and stability linked with its ability to form broad-scale enterprises capable of competing effectively in international markets. And they see the family-centered basis of Taiwan's society and businesses as sometimes detrimental to developing this ability to form enterprises capable of effective competition. A pessimistic scenario shows eventual economic slowdown and possible stagnation in Taiwan as the family-centered structure keeps the economy in the rut of small-scale enterprises. Under this scenario, a decline in prosperity would increase complaints against the government at a time of delicate transition from a mainlander-dominated administration to one with greater representation of Taiwanese which would lead to polarization and confrontation between the government and its critics.

Family division continues to break up industrial conglomerates at a time when the government is trying to concentrate capital. Family atomism results in cut-throat competition which forces family firms to go underground and cut costs by counterfeiting, and adopting myriad illegal means to stay afloat. Cutting costs at every corner leaves the island's entrepreneurs few resources to develop an indigenous research and development capacity. Finally, family

29

strategies of international dispersal cause "brain drain" and capital flight that cut into resources needed locally and undermine citizen and investor confidence in the island's economic health.

The government has taken actions that have helped to foster Taiwan's family-centered growth. Land reform, followed by rapid industrialization, increased the availability of tangible wealth, which served as the raison d'être and the structural basis for large extended families. At the same time, widespread development multiplied opportunities for sojourning, which eased the interpersonal conflicts that divided families in earlier eras. Beyond this, the unavailability of loans for small-scale entrepreneurs forced would-be entrepreneurs to rely on kinship and social networks for investment funds. Finally, the absence of public sources of social security forced families to provide their own support for the elderly and unemployed. Buttressing these and other tangible conditions favoring strong families was an official ideology, promoted in the schools and mass media, that supported Confucian values such as strong, harmonious families. Presumably, the government can modify some of these policies and take additional steps in order to both reduce the Taiwan economy's heavy reliance on family-centered development and the shortcomings of that kind of development for future economic advancement.

Class Dissent as a Source of Instability One challenge to Taiwan's family-based social stability could come from the perceived discontent of the more well-to-do middle class and the intellectuals. These people play leading roles in government and business, political, academic, and other private institutions, and they define and interpret ideology and culture in Taiwan. Most would agree that Chinese tradition and Confucian values have played an important role in defining government policy and in guiding contemporary behavior on Taiwan. They are seen as helpful in explaining how Taiwan achieved rapid economic development and social progress without the severe dislocation and instability that have accompanied such changes in other developing countries. But as Taiwan modernizes, remains separate from the Chinese mainland, and develops an increasingly outward-looking international posture, these traditional ideas could weaken. Indeed, these ideas are more closely associated with the mainlander elite, who came to Taiwan 40 years ago and who are now dying out to be replaced by leaders born and raised on Taiwan.

The values of the latter group are more mixed. In effect, these people are searching for a new identity and culture amid a mix of

30

often conflicting values introduced into the island by Chinese tradition, the Japanese occupation of 1895–1945, and the post–World War II period of close relations with the United States. Their leaders are often frustrated by Taiwan's international isolation and see its fate heavily dependent on the often unpredictable actions of outside forces, notably the government on the mainland, the United States, and Japan. They acknowledge the economic and social advances Taiwan has made, but they still search for a greater sense of national identity and dignity for themselves and their fellow residents on the island.

Social malaise need not lead to instability or other outcomes detrimental to the continued peace and prosperity of the region, but it could intensify some recent trends that have the potential to disrupt Taiwan's future stability. For example, many intellectuals in Taiwan remain dissatisfied with the Nationalist government system, with its pretensions to ruling all of China and its unwillingness to make its institutions truly representative of and accountable to the people on Taiwan. Rallying behind the call of opposition politicians for political reform, they call for sweeping changes in Nationalist government institutions that would transform them into truly representative bodies. At the extreme are intellectuals and politicians who defy the legal ban on advocating a separate status or independence for Taiwan. Independence would doubtless satisfy those in Taiwan who seek a new and separate identity. At the same time, however, it would challenge the fundamental raison d'être of the Nationalist government and would alarm the PRC, which has warned that it would use force to prevent Taiwan from breaking away from the mainland. As such, it would set the stage for possibly violent confrontation internally and externally—developments that would obviously place at risk the social stability that has been so important to Taiwan's success.

IV. Taiwan's Role in the World Economy

Economic modernization lies behind much of the important social and political changes seen in Taiwan in recent years. It has also been instrumental in defining Taiwan's international stature and U.S. interests in the island. The modernization of Taiwan's economy was neither easy nor smooth; every success brought new challenges which, if not overcome, could have hindered economic development and possibly led to political crisis and social instability.

In 1950 the Nationalists suffered from severe inflation, feared an invasion by Communist forces, and faced an angry populous. By 1952 inflation was tamed, the Communist invasion had not materialized, and Taiwanese anger was reduced by land reform and the rapid economic recovery already underway. Then, in the mid-1950s, the economy failed to create enough jobs due to a slowdown in the expansion of heavy industry. The government responded by dismantling the dual exchange-rate system in 1958 and encouraging industries to export.

Success created new problems in the mid-1960s as wages began to rise and skilled labor became scarce. The marked rise of oil prices in 1973 added to these new cost pressures. This contributed to a great rise in overall costs in some industries, which in turn began to undermine the island's trade competitiveness. By 1975 the economy had readjusted, growth had resumed, and policies had been enacted to reduce dependency upon oil imports. Even when the United States severed diplomatic relations in 1979 and a year later ended the Mutual Defense Treaty, Taiwan overcame the political shock and uncertainty and continued to develop rapidly. In 1981 a worldwide recession began to depress economic activity and increase unemployment, but by late 1983 the economy had rebounded. Per capita income had risen to nearly ten times that of the People's Republic of China, and the two-way trade between Taiwan and the United States had reached almost US$16 billion. By 1986 the growth in trade was such that the U.S. *trade deficit* with Taiwan was about the same as *total U.S. trade* with Taiwan had been in 1983. Today Taiwan is America's fifteenth largest export market and its sixth largest source of imports. Efforts to resolve past economic difficulties coincided with and influenced a major shift in the economy: Taiwan rapidly reduced its dependency on agriculture and primary-product exports and became a manufacturing society tightly linked to the world economy. This shift was achieved with a more equal distribution of wealth than other countries of comparable per capita income.

Taiwan's rapid economic transformation reflects complex relationships among economic growth, income distribution, and productivity. Private enterprise has been flexible enough to adopt new technology and facilitate resource reallocation from agriculture to industry and services, and, within manufacturing, from food processing, leather making, and textiles to electronics, machine tools, and car-assembly parts. The public sector has coordinated many of the activities of the private sector, and the state-controlled enterprises have produced vital goods and services. The dynamic interaction between the private and public sectors owes much to the state's dedicated leadership.

The Structure of Taiwan's Economy

The pattern of economic change and performance in Taiwan since the 1940s shows the remarkable success of Taiwan's enterprises in overcoming adjustment difficulties. Several factors explain this success. Although many enterprises go bankrupt each year in Taiwan, new ones take their place. There are few large corporate giants that greatly depend upon banks and the government sector for assistance, in contrast, for example, to the situation in Japan or Korea, where these kinds of large corporations are much more important. Highly competitive product and service markets characterize the Taiwan economy, with tens of thousands of small and medium-size enterprises vigorously competing in the domestic and foreign markets. Taiwanese businessmen adjust their sales and activities to prevailing prices. Their profit margins are small, and they depend on sales volume and low unit costs to make profits.

There is a pervasive business ethic in Taiwan which makes business success a source of great pride. Whereas government service was once considered to be the ideal career path, in recent years a trend has emerged in which young people would often rather go into business. As the business ethic is legitimized and widespread, so is there a great willingness of people to work hard and long, often more than 40 hours per week. Young and middle-aged people will often take two jobs to save enough money to invest in a new business. Women have entered the workforce in greater numbers, and their wages and salaries contribute to the capital of households and enterprises. The island economy now has probably the world's highest savings-to-income ratio, around 35 percent. Thus, in spite of a very undeveloped financial sector, business firms and households can still finance new activities with the funds they have saved and borrowed through their social networks.

Taiwanese also place a high premium on acquiring an education. This strong cultural trait helps explain why such a high proportion of young people are in school, stay in the classroom for long periods, and vigorously compete for the limited space in colleges and universities. Because fewer than 10 percent pass the university entrance exams each year, competition to obtain a higher education is intense. In recent years, the state has spent considerable funds to develop vocational schools to train skilled and semi-professional manpower.

Another crucial factor in the solution of economic problems over the past 30 years has been the effectiveness of the government's role in promoting economic modernization. The interaction of the public and private sector has not involved extremely large government spending (which recently has been around 24 percent of GNP) but, rather, types of government policies that have fostered innovation, nurtured flexibility in the economy, and provided encouragement and incentive. These administrative efforts have been numerous and varied, but they can be classified into three categories.

First, the government pursued policies to restructure economic incentives, particularly by the redistribution of property rights. Such policies included the government-sponsored land reform in the early fifties and reform of the foreign-exchange-rate control system in the late fifties. Second, government policies shifted resources from low to high value-added products by inducing more competition, channeling the flow of economic activity in new ways, and facilitating the role of markets. For example, there were government efforts to encourage the development of new import-substitution industries like synthetic fibers in the fifties and to set up export-processing zones in the sixties. Finally, the government inaugurated policies to achieve equilibrium within the economic system by offsetting certain kinds of scarcities. For example, there were policies in the seventies to develop infrastructure, and monetary and fiscal policies in the early eighties helped counter the negative effects of the 1981–82 recession. These and other examples of government initiative helped the private sector respond to market signals, upgrade the quality of human and physical resources, and prevent market failure.

The government remains strongly committed to using its power to facilitate economic growth through these types of policies. Although KMT and government officials recognize the great advantage of nurturing private enterprise and protecting private property, neither the party nor the government will stand aside and let market forces decide all market outcomes. The state continually intervenes in the market through new legislation and policies aimed at providing stable growth and ensuring that the gap in income distribution between rich and poor sectors of society does not widen as growth takes place. The state also strives to minimize unemployment and maintain stable price levels, responding with the market adjustments that it perceives to be necessary to achieve these ends.

Whereas in other countries government intervention has run against the dictates of the market and, in many cases, has proven counterproductive to economic development, Taiwan's government intervention has had a generally positive effect. This has been the case in large measure because the government has intervened only selectively. It has focused particularly on policies designed to advance industry into greater value-added areas, or on policies designed to weed out technologically backward industries that can no longer compete in world markets. Moreover, when determining the strengths and weaknesses of particular enterprises and an appropriate government role in helping them, the government has tended to judge them on the basis of their international competitiveness rather than by other, more subjective standards.

While the government takes an active role to help enterprises respond to new market forces, it maintains a balanced budget and refuses to resort to deficit spending for pump-priming economic growth during recession times. The central bank also tries to pursue a monetary policy to maintain steady expansion of the money supply and to keep interest rates as high as possible in order to encourage high savings. Nonetheless, new deposits are being created in the banking system, and the economy's money supply has expanded more than intended in recent years because about 55 percent of GNP is generated through exports. This is because of Taiwan's unusually favorable trade balance on current account.

Taiwan's Technology Strategy

One example of a government program that promotes development vital to Taiwan's current and future prosperity is the effort to advance high-technology industry. This is an area of keen interest for many Americans because it demonstrates how Taiwan is attempting to compete directly with the United States, Japan, and others and shows how Taiwan intends to penetrate U.S. and foreign markets in order to sell these products abroad. Also, highlighting the key role played by the Taiwan government in developing this important segment of the economy may illuminate some facets of the growing debate in the United States over the need perceived by some for a government-supported "industrial policy" in order to make U.S. products more internationally competitive.

The Taiwan government has played a role as an initiator and facilitator of programs in research and development, education, and economic restructuring. Even though the state has been committed in principle to allowing the forces of the market guide the operation of its economy and the behavior of local firms, it has often found it necessary, and at times desirable, to intervene where private-sector responsiveness was lacking or where the local economy lacked the maturity to compete effectively in the international market.

Furthermore, a critical aspect of government behavior has been policies regarding multinational firms, particularly in the area of technology transfer. In general, the state has managed to maximize the flow of foreign technology into the local economy. In many cases, the presence of foreign companies—either in terms of equity-based investment, final product and component sourcing activities, or licensing of technology—has served as a catalyst. It has set off the search for new and more efficient technologies on the part of local firms (public and private) through the demands of product end-users in overseas markets, as well as the backward and forward linkages created by foreign firms. This catalytic effect, especially when combined with Taiwan government-imposed domestic-content requirements, has set in motion the technological modernization of the country.

As certain industries experience periods of rapid technological change, where innovation-related skills in organization, management, and technology are in high demand, most third world firms have been unable to stay in the market, except perhaps at a very low end. Taiwanese firms, however, have been able to retain their positions through a combination of gradual, though steadily evolving, private-and public-sector research and development supports. It is this evolution of local capabilities—first in terms of production efficiency and more recently in terms of marketing and innovativeness—that not only explains the initial entry and competitiveness of Taiwan firms such as Tatung, but also their ability to survive in the face of rapid and sustained technological changes, most of which have their origin in the industrialized world.

There have been five main components to Taiwan's strategy for technological advance. Most critical have been the financial and tax policies, carried out by banks and state-led financial institutions and designed to encourage firms to adopt new ideas and innovations.[7] Second, a combination of policy instruments and economic incentives has been introduced in order to facilitate the diffusion of existing technology. Third, a series of related policies has been implemented to improve the process of importing technology and its utilization. In particular, taxes on technology imports have been drastically reduced, and much of the red tape formerly experienced by foreign suppliers and local recipients has gradually disappeared. Similar policies for regulating the activities of foreign firms have also been instituted in order to ensure that technology transfers are consistent with overall technological priorities. Fourth, Taiwan has made major investments in education and training, especially in the fields of engineering and science. Literacy rates among Taiwan residents are among the highest in the developing world, averaging well over 90 percent. Finally, the government has created various vehicles for the collection and dissemination of economic and technical information, making firms constantly aware of changes in market situations, foreign government policies, or other factors that could affect their competitiveness. Taken together, these factors underlie, at a macro level at least, the amalgam of technical and economic policies that have supported export expansion in the late 1960s, industrial deepening in the 1970s, and technological upgrading in the 1980s.

The focus of Taiwan's thrust into high technologies is the Hsinchu science-based industrial park. Opened in September 1980, the park serves as a catalyst in restructuring Taiwan's industry. Growth of industry depends largely on the flow of foreign investment and technology transfer, and the science park offers incentives to investors, including tax holidays, lower-than-standard company taxes, and duty-free importation of machinery, equipment, and raw materials. The goal for the 1980s is to attract a billion dollars of foreign and domestic investment for 200 companies employing 30,000 to 40,000 workers. The park seeks investment in five broad sectors: electronics and information processing, precision in-

---

[7] See Robert Wade, "The Financial Systems of East Asia: Lessons from Taiwan," *California Management Review* (Summer 1985).

struments and machinery, high-technology material sciences, energy sciences, and aeronautical and genetic engineering. Most investment applications approved so far have been in electronics and information processing.

Taiwan's leaders also entertain other goals in promoting technological advancement. One major goal has been to use the process of technological upgrading as a means to expand and extend the island's "interdependence" with key actors in the international economy. In many ways, the essence of this policy has been reflected in attempts to increase the "dependence" of transnational firms on Taiwan as a foreign investment site and as a source of sophisticated components. (This tends to raise Taiwan's unofficial status with foreign governments caught between competing pressures from Beijing and Taipei.) The other goal has been to increase the island's technological self-sufficiency through industrial deepening. Economic and political concerns about the availability of adequate energy supplies, military equipment, and other strategic goods have led the state to increase its efforts to develop an assortment of critical production technologies. Most notably, Taiwan has worked hard in recent years to develop its own fighter aircraft and other segments of its defense industry, in part because foreign governments have been unwilling to risk Beijing's displeasure by selling sophisticated weapons to Taipei.

Taiwan's Strategy in Practice

Interest on the part of foreign firms in Taiwan began to grow, albeit slowly, in the late 1960s. This was a result of the infrastructure in place and the creation of a series of investment statutes that made the island an attractive site for locating a factory, particularly for assembly types of operations where foreign companies could take full advantage of the lower-cost wage structure. In addition, the formation of the Kaohsiung and Nantze export-processing zones (EPZs), with each offering additional investment incentives, sparked further interest.

Most of the initial foreign investment, especially in the EPZs, involved little direct technology transfer. Most of the projects, which were in the light-industry category (e.g., toys, garments, consumer electronics, and food processing), involved simple assembly operations. The EPZs operated like foreign enclaves, minimizing the amount of contact between the local economy and the foreign market, except in terms of the workers who moved in and out of the zones in response to new or better employment opportunities. Over time, however, it was the mobility of the labor force that proved to be one of the main vehicles for technology and skills transfer, especially in terms of middle-level management and technical personnel. A percentage of the individuals who were trained initially to work in the zones went on to start up their own companies or brought their skills into the local economy for use in domestic firms.

As foreign investment began to increase in the mid-1960s and 1970s, so did the number of formal technical-cooperation agreements. Here again, some of the increase was a reflection of the new regulatory regime set up by the government to promote technical cooperation with foreign firms. The specific factors behind the growing interest on the part of foreign firms were twofold. First, as it became necessary to do more local sourcing, it became cost-effective as well as good business practice to help upgrade local capabilities. In some circumstances, the government "required" such assistance as part of the approval process for the establishment of a foreign-invested factory. Second, laws became more restrictive concerning capitalization of technology by foreign firms in joint ventures. This led companies to seek more formal means to obtain a direct return on their know-how.

The practices of American and Japanese companies have differed considerably in this regard. For firms from Japan, technical cooperation became a vehicle to expand the extent of Japanese vertical integration on the island. Settling for joint ventures in many cases, Japanese firms often required a technical-cooperation agreement when forming a joint venture in order to obtain an additional return on their technical know-how. According to one study, these agreements frequently did not really involve much technology transfer.[8] The study suggests that there was more evidence of "show-how" than transfer of "know-how." Technical cooperation was viewed by Japan as a means to penetrate the Taiwan economy, often using such agreements as a means to "tie up" local firms by requiring them to buy parts, components, or raw materials from the Japanese technology supplier or another Japanese equity-related firm operating in the domestic economy.

[8] Chen Ting-kuo, "The Effective Approach of Technology Cooperation with Foreign Firms" (Taipei: Metals Industry Research Laboratory, 1978) (in Chinese), cited in Denis Fred Simon, "Taiwan's Strategy for Creating Competitive Advantage: The Role of Foreign Technology," presented to The Asia Society Conference on Taiwan, April 1987.

As of 1985 even though the overall dollar value of approved U.S. investment (US$1.716 billion) was greater than that of Japan (US$1.130 billion), Japanese companies have had almost twice as many cases of foreign investment (900 versus 505). The number of technical-cooperation agreements involving Japanese firms (1,443) exceeds the number of U.S. cases (492) by a factor of three. This ratio holds even in such cases as electronics, where one study found that Japanese firms accounted for 70 percent of the technical-cooperation agreements.[9] Yet, in the case of American firms, there is general agreement that there has been much more actual technology transfer, whether through the process of direct foreign investment or through formal technology-cooperation agreements. One example is the joint venture between Ford and a Taiwan firm to produce automobiles on the island. Ford assisted several local auto-parts suppliers to upgrade the quality of their components as part of its program to increase local sourcing. Nevertheless, in essence, in spite of the differences in dollar exposure, the Taiwan economy is much more linked with Japan's economy, not only in trade relations but also apparently in terms of technology acquisition.

Prospects for Continued Economic Growth

Some economic experts caution that the newly industrializing countries (NICs) of East Asia may not be able to maintain their rapid export growth rates of the recent past, and that, therefore, because of their high foreign-trade dependency, their overall economic growth rates may begin to decline. Singapore's negative or low growth in the mid-1980s is cited as a case in point, and its difficulties are said to have broader implications for similar, export-oriented countries in the region, including Taiwan.

Taiwan's physical resources are limited. As of the mid-1980s, the agricultural sector provided less than 8 percent of net GNP; industry, around 45 percent; and services, around 47 percent. About 60 percent of the population comprised the economy's workforce; fewer than 17 percent worked in agriculture, about 42 percent worked in secondary industry, and the remainder were in services. The island's economy is heavily dependent upon foreign trade, with exports constituting around 55 percent of GNP. Taiwan's

[9] Chi Schive, "An Evaluation of Technology Acquisition in the Electronics Industry" (Taipei: Investment Commission, Ministry of Economic Affairs, September 1980) (in Chinese), cited in Denis Fred Simon, *op. cit.*

economy depends greatly on trade for the raw and finished materials with which to produce goods and services for domestic use and foreign sale. And the island is strongly dependent upon foreign trade for its supply of energy. In short, without foreign trade, Taiwan's economy would rapidly wither and die. This makes the current trend of international protectionism particularly worrisome and adds some validity to the arguments of those who see a gloomy future for Taiwan and other NICs.

Over the long run, Taiwan seeks to maintain high growth rates and high productivity, keep unemployment and inflation low, and protect its balanced income distribution. Many factors make Taiwan's prospects for achieving these goals favorable. Taiwan's business firms and households have great resiliency, are frugal, strive to be efficient and highly productive, and—perhaps most important—remain ready to respond and adapt to new market forces. It is this flexibility that should enable the economy to continue to outperform most other economies in coming decades. Given continued social and political stability and peaceful conditions along the Taiwan Strait, Taiwan should be able to upgrade productivity in its manufacturing and service sectors; continue to have high savings and make the necessary investment in new capital to improve economic performance and product quality; and maintain markets in foreign countries by which to earn the foreign exchange needed to purchase the necessary raw materials and products from abroad.

To achieve these goals, Taiwan will have to meet and overcome a number of international and domestic economic pressures. For example, increased international protectionism threatens Taiwan's export base, and Taiwan's trading partners continue to pressure for an opening of its market, appreciation of the New Taiwan dollar, and other structural reforms. Taiwan also faces the domestic challenges of an aging population and the need to develop indigenous science and technology capabilities. Moreover, there appears to be a widespread feeling of anxiety in Taiwan that the current situation is too good to last. Added to international economic worries are Taiwanese concerns over the island's political future vis-à-vis the mainland at a time of leadership transition in both Beijing and Taipei.

Nevertheless, Taiwan's economy has shown a remarkable ability to adjust in the face of new challenges and demands. There is a growing perception that Taiwan's markets are opening and operating more fairly. The longstanding ratio of the New Taiwan (N.T.) dollar to the U.S. dollar of 40:1 has now changed. The N.T. dollar has appreciated to under 30 per U.S. dollar, and is bound to appre-

41

ciate even further. What especially hurts Taiwan's position in the eyes of trading partners like the United States is Taiwan's large current foreign-reserve holdings of over US$70 billion. Proponents of protectionism in the United States cite that figure and the $19 billion annual U.S. trade deficit as grounds for retaliation.

Over the past year, the Taiwan government has taken steps to address this. It has relaxed foreign-exchange controls, allowed people on Taiwan to invest more freely abroad, and permitted the value of the N.T. dollar to rise relative to the U.S. dollar. But many of Taiwan's trading partners see these steps as only the beginning of the substantial and structural financial reforms needed. In particular, without reform, the current financial structure will generate greater foreign-reserve holdings, which are likely to bring about renewed complaints from abroad. It will also impede smooth capital formation and investment in larger-scale enterprises, which are widely seen as essential for Taiwan's ability to continue to compete in world markets. Thus, these critics urge a streamlining of Taiwan's slow-moving economic decision-making process to respond to international pressures for reform.

To deal with protectionist trends in the United States and elsewhere, Taiwan's government will have to take at least some of the following steps:

- Reduce tariffs and remove non-tariff barriers, which are often legacies of the past when Taiwan was struggling to balance her international trade account. Tariff rates are seen as too high on goods that in the past were produced domestically in the name of conserving foreign exchange but that are highly competitive today.

- Expand public investment in order to introduce more imports in such areas as public housing, schools, roads, public health, environmental protection, basic research and development, and an appropriately designed, flexible program of social welfare. (Such investment would presumably come at the expense of investment in major infrastructure for export-oriented industries, formerly a priority.)

- Appreciate Taiwan's currency to help close the trade gap through price effects. At the moment the N.T. dollar is still widely seen as undervalued. The effect of appreciation would make Taiwan's exports more expensive in terms of foreign currency (notably, U.S. dollars), thus reducing Taiwan's exports,

42

and would simultaneously make imports in Taiwan dollars less expensive, thus encouraging more imports into Taiwan.

Such reform will be complicated by the need to respond to demographic changes that will affect the nature of Taiwan's labor market. By the year 2000, Taiwan's population will have begun to age. The population growth rate has fallen to 1.1 percent per annum, and it will continue to fall as more young people postpone marriage and opt for smaller families. While only around 5 percent of the population is now over the age of 65, this proportion will more than double by the year 2000, and then it will increase even more rapidly. By the first and second decades of the new century, Taiwan will be experiencing the same problems Japan and the United States currently face in trying to provide for the aged. But even here Taiwan has certain advantages over these societies: it does not carry the massive debt that Japan and the United States now have, and Chinese families still tend to provide the needed support for the aged.

In many respects Taiwan has just begun to confront the many complex tasks that accrue to any nation wishing to participate in what has become an increasingly global competitive environment. Its desire to restructure the existing international division of labor and enter into more technologically sophisticated industries will involve major commitments of political, economic, and technological resources. Moreover, success will necessitate effective and sustained mobilization of these resources to a far greater extent than ever before. Under such circumstances, the role of the state as a strategic actor will become more important. If the past is any guide, the state is the only entity capable of aggregating discreet individual interests into a coherent whole. The Taiwan government will want to, and perhaps increasingly will be required to, pick the winners and losers, sort out the potentially successful challengers from the inefficient ones, and assist with selection of the markets and products to be targeted.

Technologically, while the private sector may respond to state encouragement and incentives for building up indigenous science and technology capacity in some respects, the stakes may allow even less room for private-sector discretion. The international market for high technology is much too dynamic to permit the Taiwan state to relinquish its role as initiator, facilitator, and regulator. Of course, the private sector will not be a mere pawn. Large, technically advanced firms in Taiwan will increasingly be able to hold their own in responding to competitive threats and capitalizing on emerging opportunities. In promoting certain domestic firms as bearers of national industrial power and prestige, Taiwan will have to be able to put forth companies that have the efficiency, flexibility, and managerial effectiveness that is required to compete in overseas markets. Unless such firms exist, Taiwan's objective to advance its position in the international division of labor will likely be unattainable.

Taiwan has taken numerous steps to strengthen the technological base upon which its present and future economic activities are based. In some cases, there appears to be a synergy developing, where local technological skills are being complemented by the participation of high-technology firms from the United States and Japan in a variety of cooperative ventures. And yet, what Taiwan is doing in the area of technology represents a fundamental challenge to the traditional notions of comparative advantage. That is, Taiwan is determined not to become too dependent on more advanced economies in order to avoid becoming highly vulnerable to the vagaries of domestic economic policy or corporate decision making in the United States, Japan, or Western Europe. Taiwan wants to diversify its sources of technology, its markets, and its products. Its ongoing efforts to enhance domestic capabilities are not designed to limit global economic exchange but to help improve the terms of Taiwan's participation in global markets.

Taiwan has not overcome its technological dependency on the industrialized world; for the most part it is still far from attaining the "offensive" level of technological capability needed to set the trend in foreign markets. At the same time, Taiwan has significantly eradicated its once near-total dependence on outside sources for technology and know-how through a process of learning by doing, local innovation, and the successful absorption of foreign technology. The experience of Taiwan strongly indicates that there is room for mobility in the international division of labor, and it reinforces very traditional notions about the use of public policy to defend and advance national economic and political interests.

In sum, Taiwan government leaders and entrepreneurs seem to understand clearly the economic problems that lie ahead. They have been altering past practices in order to position the island's economy to continue to grow amid the highly competitive international economic environment. They are well aware that they do not control this environment and that international circumstances could change and have a profound impact on Taiwan's development. Nevertheless, their recent initiatives—if carried out successfully—seem to be moving the island's economy in ways well designed to ensure continued growth and prosperity.

44

V. The Evolving Political System

While Taiwan's social stability and economic development are widely admired, its political system is much more controversial. Debate centers on the degree of "authoritarianism" in the one-party Nationalist rule: to what extent are the people on Taiwan disenfranchised by a system that continues to be dominated at its upper levels by an elite that came from mainland China 40 years ago and that still relies on political institutions carried over at that time?[10]

On one side of the debate are those who feel that the Nationalists have been lucky to avoid a major uprising. Proponents of this view maintain that as Taiwan has advanced economically and socially, the demands of the people to manage their political system have grown. Meeting with continued determination by the Nationalists to hold the major share of political power, the temporarily suppressed population is growing more discontented. It is argued that this sets the stage for a clash that could seriously jeopardize Taiwan's future stability and development.

A contrary view stresses that economic and social advancement have served to legitimize the Nationalists' rule, mitigating against majority demands for substantial changes in the Nationalist-controlled political system. Proponents also stress that the Nationalists have been adroit in gradually incorporating increasing numbers of Taiwanese into their party and in slowly easing past controls on dissidents' ability to voice their opinions and organize politically. In effect, proponents of this view judge that the government's legitimacy has rested on its ability to provide economic and social advancement for large segments of the population and to manage concurrent political demands in ways that will not be detrimental to continued economic and social progress. Political opposition forces are seen to represent only a minority, with little broad popular appeal in the absence of some major economic or other policy failure by the government.

Advocates of these and other competing perspectives on Taiwan's political system are all able to find evidence to substantiate their views because the system is complex and in the midst of ma-

---

[10] In addition to the presentations made at The Asia Society Conference on Taiwan, this section draws on a draft manuscript on the political opposition in Taiwan prepared by Alyson Pytte, Congressional Research Service, Library of Congress (September 1987).

jor change. During 1987 the Nationalists, under President Chiang Ching-kuo, began a process of reform that involved ending the 38-year martial law regime, considering an overhaul of parliamentary bodies brought over from mainland China in the 1940s, and allowing the political opposition to organize and form a viable opposition party. The incentive for change has come from several sources. Most important of these were the rising demands of opposition politicians—backed by elements of the middle class and workers—for increased opportunity to participate in the political life of Taiwan. Another factor has been the problem of leadership succession posed by the passing of President Chiang.

The Political Opposition and the Impetus for Reform

On July 14, 1987, President Chiang Ching-kuo ended martial law and agreed to lift a ban on opposition parties after 40 years of authoritarian rule. Although rival political parties remained illegal until the revision of statutes governing "civic organizations" was completed, the ruling Nationalist Party (KMT) took no steps to dismantle the island's main opposition party, the Democratic Progressive Party (DPP).

The DPP was formed from a loose coalition of non-KMT legislators and political activists known as the *tang-wai* ("party outsiders"). Prompted in part by the success of democratic movements in South Korea and the Philippines, *tang-wai* activists formally established the DPP in September 1986. At its first organizational meeting in November of that year, the DPP created a structure almost identical to that of the KMT: a 31-member Central Executive Committee was elected for two years with powers to appoint an eleven-member Central Standing Committee and a chairman, both for one-year terms. Unlike the KMT, however, the DPP granted little control to the chairman, and the party is carefully designed to prevent over-centralization of power. Also, new members must be nominated by at least three current members, apparently to prevent one opposition faction (or the KMT) from controlling the DPP through aggressive membership recruitment.

Despite pressure from right-wing groups and conservative elements within the KMT, Chiang Ching-kuo took no formal repressive action against the DPP. In December 1986 DPP candidates campaigned in legislative elections and doubled their representation in the country's highest parliamentary organs: the DPP won 18.9 percent of the vote for the National Assembly, electing 11 of

46

its 25 candidates, and 22.17 percent of the vote for the Legislative Yuan, electing 12 of its 19 candidates. For the first time, DPP labor-union representatives defeated two KMT candidates in contests for occupation-based National Assembly seats.[11]

However, the DPP has displayed internal generational and ideological divisions.[12] The "New Movement" faction within the party's Standing Committee, which has its roots in the militant pre–DPP Writers and Editors Association, favors mass action over electoral politics. Although its goals are reformist, this faction calls for alliance with the working class rather than with the opposition's traditional base of support in the Taiwanese middle class. Members of this faction argue that the KMT has run an authoritarian state for four decades and will not change without pressure from street demonstrations and possibly a Philippines-style uprising. The members of this faction, including former DPP chairman Chiang P'eng-chien and DPP members Ch'iu Yi-jen, Hong Ch'i-ch'ang, and Wu Nai-jen, are among the youngest in the party.

New Movement activists are critical of the older, "moderate" faction, led by veteran legislator K'ang Ning-hsiang, for compromising too much with the KMT. An anti-K'ang campaign led by members of the activist faction was in fact largely responsible for K'ang losing an election for the Legislative Yuan in 1983. He has since regained his seat, but tension between these two groups remains. K'ang's allies on the DPP Standing Committee include legislator Fei Hsi-p'ing and provincial assemblymen Su Chen-ch'ang, You Hsi-k'un, and Chou Ts'ang-yuan. In general, members of this faction support working within the legislative system to accomplish many of the same goals advocated by New Movement activists.[13]

Providing some link between these opposing factions are DPP Central Standing Committee member and legislator You Ching, Taipei city councilman Hsieh Ch'ang-ting, and former political prisoner Yao Chia-wen. Elected DPP chairman in late 1987, Yao Chia-wen is a human-rights lawyer and one of the so-called Kaohsiung Eight—those arrested and imprisoned as a result of the Kaohsiung Incident of 1979. (A major clash between opposition

[11] For discussion of the opposition movement and the KMT response, see Yang-sun Chou and Andrew Nathan, "Democratizing Transition in Taiwan," *Asian Survey* 27 (March 1987), pp. 277–99.

[12] For background, see Jurgen Domes, "Political Differentiation in Taiwan: Group Formation Within the Ruling Party and the Opposition Circles, 1979–1980," *Asian Survey* 21 (October 1981), pp. 1011–28; Chou and Nathan, "Democratizing Transition," *op. cit.*; and weekly coverage of Taiwan in the *Far Eastern Economic Review*.

[13] *Far Eastern Economic Review* 139:4 (January 29, 1988), pp. 18–24.

demonstrators and police, the Kaohsiung Incident of 1979 was followed by the arrest, trial, and detention by the government of senior opposition leaders, including Mr. Yao.) Yao has remained largely untarnished by the ideological split between moderate and activist factions that emerged while he was in jail.

Opinion is divided over whether the DPP will hold together, at least for the short term, or will split into a number of competing parties. On August 10, 1987, Wang Yi-hsiung, one of the DPP's eleven central advisory members, announced that he would soon set up his own party to "fight for the rights of the labor force and protect their interests."[14] The New Labor Party was formed on December 5, 1987, by a small group of intellectuals and labor activists. This step underlined the divisions among opposition politicians. It remained unclear whether this new party, the DPP, or some other organization would give new political voice to Taiwan's growing industrial work force.

There was speculation that Chang Chun-hung and Huang Hsin-chieh, both recently released Kaohsiung Incident figures who refused to join the DPP, would also draw support away from the party. Chang later announced his intention to join the DPP, however. Huang, in speeches around the island, reportedly encouraged people to join the DPP while insisting that he himself played a more important role as an independent agitating for democratization of the opposition party structure.

The Opposition Platform Despite conflict between opposing factions and personalities about how reform should be accomplished in Taiwan, the majority of DPP members share these common goals:

- complete renewal of membership to the assemblies through elections;

- release of political prisoners;

- freedom of the press, freedom to establish new political parties, and freedom of assembly and demonstration;

- accelerated admission of native Taiwanese to positions of political power;

- popular election of the governor of Taiwan province and the mayors of Taipei and Kaohsiung, who are now appointed by

[14] "Split Looms in Democratic Progressive Party," BBC Summary of World Broadcasts (London: British Broadcasting Corp., August 11, 1987).

48

the central government;

- repeal of the National Security Law; and
- divestment of KMT business interests.

Of these issues, legislative reform and the National Security Law are the most pressing and controversial.

The DPP groups its agenda for legislative reform under the umbrella term of "self-determination." For moderate members of the DPP, self-determination means greater political power for the majority of Taiwanese, to be accomplished by equitable campaigns, open elections, and divestment of KMT business interests. Other members of the DPP assert—at least implicitly—that the Taiwanese electorate would abandon the goal of reunification if given a choice. In this view, self-determination could be seen as a veiled call for Taiwan independence. Advocates of both positions support opening the legislative seats controlled by mainlanders to a vote (retaining, perhaps, some symbolic representation for mainland Chinese constituencies) and instituting direct presidential elections. This, DPP members argue, is the way to accurately reflect the interests of the island's majority Taiwanese population.

Although the KMT has promised some type of legislative reform, most analysts believe the format for nominations and elections will continue to assure the KMT of a majority. The reason most often cited for this is the need to maintain national security. A DPP majority, KMT officials argue, would lead to slashes in the defense budget and would open Taiwan to Communist takeover. In particular, they note, Beijing leaders have said they may resort to force if Taiwan moves to declare independence.

Another aspect of the DPP's agenda for legislative reform involves divestment of the ruling party's extensive business interests in media, electronics, and finance. The KMT does not accept donations, and these investments are the main source of the party's finances and, in the DPP view, pose questions about conflict of interest.[15]

DPP members have also pushed for reform of the electoral system. Candidates are allowed only fifteen-day campaign periods, their expenditures are limited, they are prohibited from holding joint rallies or other activities with like-minded candidates, and they are denied access to the mass media. Although newspapers

[15] Julia Leung, "Lagging Reforms Irk Taipei's Opposition," *Asian Wall Street Journal* (July 7, 1987).

49

have begun to commit some space to covering opposition politics, television and radio remain the exclusive domain of the KMT. These electoral laws are now under revision, but the KMT will probably retain important advantages, given their superior organization and access to financial support and the media.[16] More restrictive than these campaign restraints, DPP members argue, is the threat of prosecution of candidates who express political views contrary to the KMT's anti-Communist, one-China policy under article two of the National Security Law.

The National Security Law was enacted by the government as martial law was lifted and is the second major item on the DPP's agenda for reform. The KMT says the law, which upholds some of the restrictions in force under martial law, is necessary because of the continued military threat from Beijing. Yet the law also sets new ground rules for political activity and satisfies conservative members of the KMT who oppose a loosening of authoritarian control. With the end of martial law, the role of the military in governing and punishing civilians for sedition and other crimes was ended. Civilians are no longer tried in military courts and thus are entitled to immediate defense and public proceedings. Many responsibilities of the Garrison Command, including censorship and border control, have been transferred to civilian authorities.[17]

The DPP fought passage of the National Security Law. Twelve opposition DPP legislators boycotted the final hearings of the law on July 21, 1987 with a sit-down protest, dismissing it as "old wine in a new bottle." On the same day, about 40 political prisoners held on Taiwan's Green Island began a seven-day hunger strike to protest the law. On July 12, DPP supporters demonstrated against the bill outside parliament and clashed with right-wing demonstrators (who possibly were backed by conservative members of the KMT), leading to several arrests and convictions. The DPP's main objection to the law is article two, which states that "no person may violate the constitution or advocate communism or the division of the national territory in the exercise of the people's freedoms of assembly and association"—the so-called three principles. As of yet, it is unclear how the KMT will enforce this law, but some analysts believe it could be used to dis-

---

[16] *Elections in Taiwan, December 6, 1986: Rules of the Game for the "Democratic Holiday,"* Asia Watch Report (New York: Asia Watch, November 1986).

[17] For discussion of National Security Law provisions, see "Legislative Yuan Approves National Security Law," *Taipei CNA* (in English), *Foreign Broadcast Information Service, China Daily Report* (June 24, 1987); Carl Goldstein, "Ruling Rights Retained," *Far Eastern Economic Review* (July 30, 1987); and Trong R. Chai, "Taiwan Abolished Martial Law but Leaves Loopholes," *Asian Wall Street Journal* (August 17, 1987).

band the DPP and any other opposition party advocating independence or self-determination. In any event, as more radical opposition-
ists have pressed publicly for the right to call for Taiwan's
self-determination, they have been dealt with firmly by the central authorities, with a few such advocates receiving long prison sentences.

Succession and the Impetus for Reform

Pressures for reform became more urgent in recent years in light of
the impending death of President Chiang Ching-kuo. Upon
Chiang's death in January 1988, Vice President Lee Teng-hui, a native of Taiwan and a Cornell-trained agronomist, took over as head
of state and acting chairman of the KMT.[18] He will serve out the remainder of Chiang's term, which ends in 1990. Lee Huan, who
was appointed secretary-general of the Kuomintang in July 1987, is
another key figure in the new administration. He is a long-time
supporter of a process whereby native Taiwanese have been promoted to positions in government formerly held by mainlanders.
He is reportedly well-connected in top and middle levels of the Nationalist Party and is pushing hard for more political reform. Nevertheless, the reformers run up against the more conservative inclinations of many older members of the KMT's Standing Committee,
and there is also said to be opposition to rapid reform on the part
of leading military and national security figures.

Chiang prepared for the succession. Over the last decade he had
incorporated increasing numbers of Taiwanese into key party and
administration positions. These appointments were seen as part of
Chiang's effort to ensure legal and peaceful succession by broaden-
ing the KMT's appeal among the majority Taiwanese population.
Chiang also announced his intention not be replaced by a family
member or a military regime and removed or isolated potential successors from both groups. He allowed the opposition some freedom of movement, though it is still far from being strong enough
to challenge the power of the KMT. At times, Chiang cracked
down on dissident activity, as during the period following the
Kaohsiung Incident of 1979. But on the whole, President Chiang
moved forward with more liberal policies in such areas as allowing
Taiwanese to hold power within the KMT and permitting a political
opposition to organize and function.

[18] As of this writing, a new chair was scheduled to be chosen at the KMT's Thirteenth Party Congress on July 7, 1988.

Chiang's steps toward liberalization were in part a response to demands for reform from the growing and increasingly politicized Taiwanese middle class. Chiang was also under pressure internationally—particularly from the United States—to democratize. This pressure intensified in 1984 when the head of Taiwan's Defense Ministry Intelligence Bureau was implicated in the assassination of U.S. businessman and writer Henry Liu, who wrote an unauthorized biography of Chiang. The government's image was further tarnished the following year after the bankruptcy of the Tenth Credit Cooperative led to the resignation of two cabinet ministers and revealed corruption and ineptitude among top party and government officials. It is still unclear how far the KMT wants to take reform and whether or not recent liberalization will survive the loss of Chiang's leadership. It is widely assumed that as president Lee Teng-hui will not have the preeminent power Chiang exercised; he will have to share power with others to a greater extent. Chiang's efforts at reform and liberalization prompted strong opposition among elderly legislators, conservative mainlanders in the Party Central Committee and military, and some economic technocrats.[19] Mechanisms remain for a coalition of these groups to reverse the reforms in the event of violence, a succession crisis, or growing calls for Taiwan independence.

Martial law could, for example, be reenacted at any time by the president without legislative approval. The new National Security Law also contains provisions that could, depending on interpretation, be used to ban emerging political parties and repress dissent. Revisions of the electoral law, the civic organizations law, the publications law, and the legislature have been promised, but how extensive these changes will be remains unclear. The KMT has shown a loosening of its restrictions recently by allowing citizens to visit relatives in the People's Republic of China and by dropping a ban on imports of Chinese herbal medicines and some literary and scientific works. However, the government has not officially abandoned its "three no's" policy toward the PRC—no compromise, no contact, and no negotiation.

Prospects for Continued Political Stability

Several major factors will determine whether President Lee Teng-hui will be able to maintain political stability or whether the

[19] See, for example, Shim Jae Hoon, "The Legacy of Reform," *Far Eastern Economic Review* 139:4 (January 29, 1988), pp. 18-19.

leadership transition will be interrupted (e.g., by a major KMT crackdown on political expression or a victory by the political opposition in gaining majority power). Perhaps most important will be the attitude of the majority of people on Taiwan concerning the limits on their political rights under the present system. From one perspective, their demands for political participation have increased less than many outside observers expected. Indeed, those who hold that growing economic wealth and social and educational advancement inevitably lead to greater demands for more political participation and control might be surprised by the limited tensions in this area in Taiwan, at least up to the present. Of course, there have been some demands for expanded political participation, but on the whole the Nationalist leadership has proven remarkably adept at adjusting political institutions to absorb and/or selectively to repress these demands. A good example is the government's strategy in the elections of late 1986: it narrowly restricted the opportunities for campaigning and limited the number of seats at stake so as to ensure continued KMT dominance, yet it also allowed opposition politicians to speak out on many sensitive issues and to rack up big victories in selected races.

Moreover, President Chiang Ching-kuo devoted himself to reconciling political tensions. In particular, Chiang was careful to maintain a balance between the aging mainlander elite and the Taiwanese supporters within the KMT, gradually passing greater authority to the Taiwanese. Chiang also was careful to maintain a stable balance among potential successors, preventing one person representing a particular governmental or institutional constituency from gaining dominant power at the expense of others. Chiang's practices clouded the predictions of those who wished to see a clearly designated successor, but they continually rejuvenated and reformed the administrative structure of the Nationalist regime. Of course, the major drawback of this successful strategy is that the new president, Lee Teng-hui, does not have the personal power he may need to deal with complicated internal and international difficulties in the period ahead. He will depend, in part, on the cooperation or at least acquiessence of other senior Taiwan leaders.

Political tensions on Taiwan may also be held in check by Taiwan's international political and economic environment and by its Chinese sociocultural heritage. Taiwan's domestic political development is constrained by its position in global geopolitics and the global economy, both of which seem to require some democracy but not too much. Any radical redefinition of domestic political legitimacy could entail an equally radical redefinition of Taiwan's international political status. In particular, a wholesale abandonment of Taipei's claim to be the legitimate government of China and the establishment of a formally separate status for the island government might be satisfying to some politicians critical of the current political system on the island, but it probably would not be supported by Taiwan's friends abroad and could provoke intervention by the People's Republic.

At the same time, many Americans with an interest in Taiwan encourage progress toward more democracy on the Western model. The situation has been complicated by the fact that some American politicians have strongly identified themselves with the demands of the political opposition in Taiwan, while others advocate strong continued support for the more gradual reform efforts of the ruling Nationalist administration. Both the KMT and the opposition conduct powerful and effective lobbying efforts in the United States which keep their respective supporters active and concerned.

Economically, any appearance of domestic political instability could affect the flow of trade, investment, and technology on which Taiwan's domestic prosperity depends. On the other hand, many foreign businessmen believe that gradually increased political participation for the population on Taiwan is more likely to produce a disciplined work force and stable investment climate than will heavy-handed repression. This, too, encourages the maintenance of some combination of authoritarianism and democracy. Such external exigencies continue to provide impressive arguments against drastic domestic political change, arguments that even some opposition leaders accept in part.

Taiwan's Chinese sociocultural heritage is also seen to strongly condition both the extent of pressure for political change and the interplay among political elites. Taiwan's formal political institutions are relatively recent imports from abroad, grafted onto traditional Chinese values of deference to age, cultivation of networks, and preference for mediation over confrontation. It remains important to reconcile policy measures and personnel appointments with these informal values as well as with constitutional forms. On Taiwan, for example, it remains of practical political significance that the president is obliged to show elaborate solicitude for loyal former associates and that subordinates feel compelled to demonstrate their loyalty. Conversely, ambitious subordinates can amass power through quiet network building, although President Chiang's habit was periodically to cut down to size anyone who overreached himself. Taiwan may owe much of its political and economic success to such tempering values.

Sources of Future Political Tension

In light of the recent political initiatives of both the Nationalist government and the opposition Democratic Progressive Party, it seems fair to conclude that Taiwan's political system is likely to become more liberalized and democratic. What may be needed now is a set of new rules and fresh formulas for reallocating political power and public resources. In order to foster a course of stable development, these rules and formulas will need to meet the opposition's rising expectations without causing severe damage to the vested interests of the beneficiaries of the current system. In short, the task will involve complicated compromise among contending political forces. A general consensus will be required on the pace of liberalization and democratization. Failure to strike an appropriate balance between change and stability could trigger a process of prolonged struggle between the proponents and opponents of recent political reforms, possibly leading to violence. In that case, instead of a smooth transition toward democracy, political development could lock into a vicious cycle of action and reaction along the path of disorder and repression.

Looking toward the 21st century, one sees at least three broad political issues that may shape the future evolution of Taiwan's political system:

- institutional changes involving the ruling Nationalist Party's relationships with both the state and society;

- political succession and composition of political leadership; and

- legitimacy of Taipei as the government of China.

Party, State, and Society The political foundation of the Taiwan government is essentially an authoritarian, one-party state. Its overall organizational structure bears strong resemblance to the Leninist system, minus Marxist ideology. The ruling Nationalist Party, or KMT, views itself as a missionary revolutionary party with a professed goal of national unification with the mainland. As the guiding ideology it adopts *San Min Chu-i* (Three People's Principles), doctrines originally put forth by the party's founding father, Sun Yat-sen. The party's decision-making and operational code are

heavily influenced by the Leninist doctrine of democratic central-
ism, which the party expressly adopted during the course of its re-
organization in 1950–52. At first glance, such a party would appear
not to be well-suited to function as a democratic party. Yet, over
the decades, it has adapted in structure and policy to many
changes that have taken place in Taiwan. The issue at the moment
is no longer whether the KMT is susceptible to change, but what
kind of change it could accept without putting its governing position at risk.

Under the existing political system, the KMT and the state are often inseparable. In general, the party establishes primacy over the
state in most aspects of policy and personnel matters, with major
issues in these areas handled by the party's Central Standing Committee. The party forms cell and branch organizations in all aspects
and at all levels of the government administration, the judiciary,
the armed forces, and the legislatures. Through these branches and
cells, the party enforces political loyalty. Practically all leaders in
these state institutions are party members. Political careers of the
party members show substantial crossover between party and state
positions, and state funds have been channeled into the support of
party-related activities.

In short, to separate party from state in Taiwan will be an extremely difficult process. But the extent to which such a separation
is made will affect the nature of political development, and strong
democratic development will necessitate that party and state be dif-
ferentiated in two ways: by function and in the career patterns of
the political elites. Such separation has occurred on a limited scale.
The party has given the technocrats virtual autonomy in the financial and economic sectors since the 1950s. Since the 1970s the party
has shown additional restraint in dealing with government administration. Recently, it has announced its intention to close down
party offices on college campuses. Nevertheless, the party still
maintains an extensive network of interlocking relationships with
state institutions, and the relationship between the Nationalist
party-state regime and society in Taiwan remains close. Organized
groups, schools, and the mass media are looked upon as part of
the regime and are treated as "transmission belts" of party-state
ideas and instructions. In specific fields such as labor, selected organized groups are given a virtual monopoly in representation by
the regime, and the party exerts considerable control over selection
of the groups' leaders and articulation of their demands.

The Taiwan government's continued use of this approach may
present a severe structural handicap for the future evolution of po-

litical pluralism and democratic development. Registered associations in Taiwan increased from about 2,500 in 1952 to almost 9,800 by 1983, when they had about 5.6 million members, or 28 percent of the population. Proliferation of these groups and associations is largely the function of Taiwan's rapid socioeconomic development. The largest and the most resourceful of these groups—the trade unions, the farmers' associations, industrial and commercial associations, water-irrigation associations, and teachers' associations—are seen as strongly influenced by the Nationalist Party through political spoils, rules manipulation, and the party's organizational penetration. New groups formed in the society—particularly those formed by small businesses, professionals, and activists on such issues as the environment or consumer protection—enjoy a greater degree of autonomy in articulating their interests as well as in lobbying and public education. However, a majority of them shy away from backing non–Nationalist Party candidates for public offices, and some observers see their political autonomy as restricted.

Thus, Taiwan is experiencing a difficult transition from a restrictive to a more pluralistic approach to social and political organization. As long as the existing restrictive approach remains, liberalization in Taiwan will be limited, and political development, even with a continuing of the recent trend of democratization, is not likely to follow the path of pluralistic democracy. The Nationalist party-state will likely remain reluctant to re-orient its relationship with the society, and short of revolutionary change, sociopolitical autonomy of secondary associations will evolve only gradually over time.

Leadership Taiwan is accustomed to "strongman politics." Since 1949 the party-state in Taiwan has had only two strong leaders, President Chiang Ching-kuo, who served from 1978 until his death in January 1988, and his father, President Chiang Kai-shek, who served from 1949 to 1975. Both were the undisputed leaders of the country during their tenure, and concentration of power in their hands contributed to the island's political stability in the sense that serious power struggles among rival elites were held in check. Such a highly paternalistic power structure will probably show serious shortcomings now that the fatherly figure is no longer around, and major personnel and policy matters will be subject to collective decisions. No single leader has the reputation, power base, and popular following needed to emerge as an immediate successor to Chiang.

Several possibilities may occur. First, the succession issue could still touch off a power struggle, but this seems unlikely as the ruling elites share a strong consensus to avert serious political instability in the face of both the perceived threat from the Communist mainland and the potential for internal violence. From an institutional standpoint, the Nationalist Party Central Standing Committee could function as the highest council for important policy and personnel issues. But the Cabinet, the Ministry of National Defense, and perhaps the National Security Council may become even more important centers of power as the presidential office loses much of the power it had under Chiang. In the post-Chiang era, the president might not simultaneously hold the party leadership title. This would create the possibility of a triumvirate collective leadership consisting of the president, the party chairman, and the premier. As central power would no longer be concentrated, the three secretaries-general of the KMT Central Standing Committee, the National Security Council, and the President's Office, together with the top military leadership, could join the nucleus of such a collective leadership.

To create a workable collective leadership will require considerable political skill and wisdom on the part of contending figures who will be jockeying for power. The legitimacy of the successsion will depend on a careful balancing of important political variables, including the balance in the government of Taiwanese and mainlanders, the age of the new leadership, and the role of the military.

The ratio between mainlanders and Taiwanese will have to be properly adjusted to give the appearance of powersharing. Chiang Ching-kuo had already begun to move in this direction in the early 1970s. For instance, the percentage of Taiwanese in the KMT Central Standing Committee steadily increased from 14 percent in 1973 to 44 percent in 1987; of the 31 members, 14 are Taiwanese. In the Cabinet, Chiang appointed Taiwanese to head the Ministries of Interior, Communications, and more recently Justice. The posts of vice-president, vice-premier, presidents of Judicial and Control Yuan, and provincial governor were all assigned to Taiwanese in successive steps. But the crucial posts in party, defense, security, finance, foreign affairs, and economic affairs were still largely exclusive of the Taiwanese. Some adjustments in the future appointments to these posts could help enhance political unity. Outside observers see the Thirteenth KMT Party Congress (to be held in July 1988) as a possible indicator of further development in this regard.

The age of the leadership is also important. Taiwan has an unusually large number of old leaders at the upper echelon of the party-state power structure. Of the 31 members in the Central Standing Committee, two-thirds are 70 years of age or older; among them seven are at least 80 years old. About 1,000 members of the three national representative bodies, or approximately two-thirds of the total, are over 70 years of age. These old leaders followed the Nationalist government to Taiwan and have held various offices in the party and government institutions since 1949. Such a gerontocracy presents at least two problems for the political system: the upward mobility of the younger and more energetic officials is blocked, and the current leadership will virtually disappear from the political scene by the year 2000. Presently, few of the upper and the upper-middle officials are between 55 and 70 years old; most of the upwardly mobile officials are in their 40s and lower 50s. Between the old leaders and this younger elite group, there exists considerable disparity in terms of experience, career orientation, and political awareness. And, while the old guards have a strong commitment to national unification with the mainland, the younger ones—who were educated and grew up in Taiwan—have fewer emotional ties with the mainland.

The third critical factor in determining the legitimacy of the succession is the role of the military. Given the KMT tradition, the military leaders have always played an important role in governing. In the 1950s and 1960s military generals were premiers and governors; they also held a substantial number of seats in the party's Central Standing Committee. Under the emergency decrees of 1949, the military extended their power into a broadly defined national security arena. Since the early 1970s, the military has reduced its presence in both the party and the government's civil administration. The recent lifting of martial law is a further step in this direction. As long as President Chiang was in charge, there was little likelihood of an abrupt reversal in the party-state's demilitarization trend. But there is less certainty about the intentions of senior military leaders in the post-Chiang period.

The top military leaders today are modern professional soldiers with training and career background in modern warfare and weaponry. The military in Taiwan, as powerful as it seems, is not a dominant institution for exercising political power as in many third world states such as South Korea, Indonesia, Iraq, and even the Philippines. Taiwan has been governed by what is probably the most effective and most well-organized political party outside the Communist world. There is no reason to expect the ruling party to take a back seat in the post-Chiang governing structure. Powerful military generals might gain pivotal positions in the party, but only if the civilian leadership fails to stabilize and a power struggle becomes inconclusive. Continuing tension with the PRC and fear of potential internal unrest may justify the military's intervention in non-military affairs. An outright military dictatorship seems remote at this point, although the future collective leadership must make room for the generals. Government and party leaders, in order to govern effectively, will need their cooperation.

Legitimacy China's unfinished civil war and the Nationalist leaders' intention to recover the mainland have been important sources of legitimacy for the Nationalist regime. As time passes and the chances of recovering control over the mainland fade, such rationalizations have begun to seem antiquated. In recent years, the administration has relied more on expanding popular elections and improving governmental performance to provide legitimacy. While elections were held only at local levels in the 1950s and the 1960s, since the 1970s elections have included seats in the national parliament, and the number of seats up for election has been steadily on the rise. In addition, legislative bills and budgets have been given more careful scrutiny in the legislatures. The recently announced parliamentary reforms announced by the KMT in February 1988 promise to phase out the old mainlanders and to make the legislature more representative of Taiwan's electorate.

However, there are serious problems of legitimacy for the Nationalists that may be beyond solution in the foreseeable future. One is Taiwan's uncertain relationship, or lack of a relationship, with the mainland. Theoretically, the Taipei regime will continue to claim to represent all of China, including the mainland, hence justifying its current institutional order and national power structure. But as the state of political separation continues, Taiwan will function more like an independent political entity rather than a rival regime of China. Such a state of affairs will keep alive the heated debate on the island regarding the proper jurisdiction of the regime, a debate that has already generated widespread partisan interest.

In short, the death of Chiang Ching-kuo has compelled the new Taiwan leaders to face domestic and international challenges with somewhat less assurance regarding their political standing in the party, government, and military. As they strive to chart the proper course for Taiwan in the sometimes difficult circumstances vis-à-vis the mainland government, the United States, and the people on Taiwan, they will be required as well to give very close scrutiny to how their policy choices will affect their leadership position in the Taiwan administration.

VI. Taiwan's International Role

Taiwan suffered a series of major diplomatic setbacks in the 1970s which culminated in the breaking of relations with the United States in 1979. Only about twenty nations now recognize the Taipei government. Among them, only South Korea, Saudi Arabia, South Africa, and the Holy See possess significant international status. Yet Taiwan's international status has improved modestly in the 1980s, and specialists point to a combination of several factors to explain this improvement: the actions of and balance of power among the major countries in Asia, the politics and policies of the PRC, and Taiwan's growing global economic stature.

The Balance of Power in Asia

During the 1980s the balance of power in Asia seemed to shift in a direction more favorable to the United States, Japan, and their friends, including Taiwan. To be sure, the Soviet Union continued efforts of the previous decade to use military-backed initiatives to expand its influence, but most Asian countries remained uninterested or fearful. They tended to group together with the United States, China, and others in order to check the spread of Soviet penetration. At the same time, Soviet officials faced serious internal problems associated with the leadership succession following Leonid Brezhnev's death in 1982 and with flagging economic development. The result was a more cautious Soviet policy, designed more to accommodate regional interests than to seek advantage through serious disruption of the prevalent balance of influence. This policy change seems to have enhanced regional stability and assisted those Asian states, including Taiwan, that appeared to have little to gain from forceful change in the regional geopolitical status quo.

The concurrent preoccupation of the People's Republic of China with internal development also seemed to be advantageous from Taiwan's perspective. It appears to have reduced the likelihood of provocative PRC policy toward the island. The objectives of PRC foreign policy in East Asia, and Chinese foreign policy generally, continues to be determined by a small group of top-level leaders who reflect the broad interests of the Chinese state as well as their own parochial concerns. The primary concerns of these leaders have been to guarantee Chinese national security, maintain internal order, and pursue economic development. Especially since the death of Mao Zedong in 1976, the priority of top leaders has been to promote successful economic modernization, which they see as the linchpin of their success or failure, and they have geared China's foreign policy to help the modernization effort. But, in order to accomplish economic modernization as well as to maintain national security and internal order, PRC leaders recognize the fundamental prerequisite of establishing a relatively stable strategic environment, especially around the nation's periphery in Asia. The alternative would be a highly disruptive situation requiring much greater Chinese expenditures on national defense and posing greater danger to domestic order and tranquility. Although the PRC has influenced this environment, it is still controlled and influenced more by others, especially the superpowers and their allies and friends. As a result, PRC leaders have been required repeatedly to assess their surroundings for changes that could affect Chinese security and development interests. And they have been compelled to adjust foreign policy to take account of such changes.

At the same time, PRC leaders have nationalistic and ideological objectives regarding irredentist claims (notably Taiwan) and a desire to stand independently in foreign affairs as a leading force among "progressive" nations of the third world. These goals have struck a responsive chord politically inside China. Occasional leadership discussion and debate over these and other questions regarding foreign affairs have sometimes had an effect on the course of Chinese foreign policy, as they did most notably during the Cultural Revolution. However, since the 1970s, the debates have become progressively less important as sources of possible change in foreign policy, and the foreign policy differences raised in them have become more moderate. In this context, nationalistic and ideological objectives regarding issues like Taiwan have generally been given secondary priority when they are in conflict with the dominant objectives of national development and security. Thus, as part of its effort to build international support for its modernization program, Beijing has sought to expand ties with the United States, Japan, and other neighboring non-Communist countries, while playing down differences with them. For many, this so-called independent foreign policy of peace has indeed contributed to peace throughout the region.

Perhaps of most importance to Taiwan, the United States has appeared more confident and powerful in Asia in recent years—a contrast with the decade of U.S. withdrawal from the region during the 1970s following the Vietnam War. A strong consensus has emerged in the United States regarding the need to keep sufficient military power in East Asia in order to help maintain a balance of influence that would check Soviet or Soviet-backed advance and re-assure U.S. allies and friends in the region. Increased U.S. confi-dence vis-à-vis the Soviet Union has been translated into a relative decline in past U.S. interest in using military and other relations with the PRC as a major source of strategic leverage—a "China card" in global competition with the Soviet Union. Although U.S.–PRC military ties have continued to develop, they and other Sino-American relations have progressed at a gradual and deliber-ate pace that has not alarmed other American friends in the region, including Taiwan.

U.S. officials also have been less likely to accommodate PRC de-mands for cutbacks in U.S. support for Taiwan in sensitive areas, notably the supply of military arms. Although the Reagan adminis-tration has continued a slow cutback in annual supply of weapons, consistent with the 1982 U.S.–PRC communiqué on the issue, the U.S. weapons transferred annually to Taiwan still are valued at around $700 million. Moreover, key areas of new military technol-ogy have appeared to be entering Taiwan's armed forces through other means, including the development of indigenous manufactur-ing ventures backed by U.S. commercial advice and equipment. For example, Taiwan's government, assisted by U.S. commercial con-tractors without U.S. government connections, has been making good progress in developing a new and highly capable fighter air-craft for Taiwan's air force. The plane is expected to be a mainstay in Taiwan's security plans vis-à-vis the mainland for the 1990s and beyond.

This regional power configuration has provided a generally fa-vorable environment for Taiwan by decreasing the friction between Taiwan and the mainland. The quest for peace and the stress on economic growth on the part of previously more provocative Com-munist states has fit in well with Taiwan's overall strategy for de-velopment. And the internal strife in South Korea and the Philip-pines has put Taiwan's political stability in a favorable light internationally. Furthermore, as noted earlier, a U.S. administration that is more confident in its dealings with the Soviet Union is less inclined to play the "China card," thus creating fewer uncertainties in the minds of the people on Taiwan. All of these developments have helped to sustain Taiwan's confidence in its own future.

The Politics and Policies of the PRC

The second set of factors behind decreased tension between Taiwan and the PRC has to do with the PRC's politics and policy, as illustrated in the discussion above. However favorable its international environment, Taiwan is directly affected by changes in policy on the mainland. During recent years, the PRC has not ceased to put pressure on Taiwan to establish ties and eventually to reunify with the mainland, sometimes directly and other times via Washington and certain international organizations. But the PRC's need to promote the Four Modernizations has required that it maintain an image, if not of a peace-lover, at least of a nation with peaceful intentions. And the PRC leadership has been aware of the subtle linkage between the Hong Kong issue and the Taiwan issue; that is, a heavy-handed approach toward one will inevitably damage the prospects for successfully handling the other. Furthermore, news of Taiwan's economic success has spread farther and deeper into the Chinese mainland, making a policy based on threats of force more difficult to justify on PRC national interest grounds.

In short, Beijing has found little advantage in a hard-line policy in the absence of a direct provocation from Taiwan. Its tone toward Taiwan has remained soft in recent years. Its aim has been not to coerce but to cajole Taipei with a variety of proposals for contacts, negotiations, or other interactions. Beijing focuses its message on both the ruling Nationalist Party and the opposition Democratic People's Party. It tries to build contacts with both while precluding any tendency by the DPP or others to move Taiwan toward independence. At the same time, Beijing's generally soft but insistent efforts regarding greater contacts and eventual reunification with Taiwan serve to reassure other Asian countries and the United States of China's peaceful intent. Beijing's approach, of course, is contingent on Taiwan taking no formal action to break with the mainland and on prospects remaining open for greater mainland-Taiwan contacts and possible negotiations. For Taiwan, the perceived threat from the PRC thus has become less urgent, though it is perhaps no less real. The PRC–British agreement of 1984 over Hong Kong served to highlight Beijing's "one country, two systems" approach to reunification with Taiwan. It added to a sense of anxiety on the part of many in Taiwan, in the KMT and DPP alike, that dealing with Beijing's insistent overtures will prove to be a major challenge in the period ahead.

Quite conscious of the possibility of change in PRC policy and the international environment, Taiwan officials have taken care not to provoke the PRC directly, nor to upset the evolving U.S.–PRC relationship. And when necessary, Taipei has adopted a flexible approach, walking a thin line between legitimacy and practicality. For instance, Taiwan participated in the 1984 Olympic Games held in Los Angeles under the name "Chinese Taipei," even though conservatives in Taiwan thought this compromised Taipei's position as the legal government of all of China. Taiwan protested Beijing's entry into the Asian Development Bank, of which Taipei is a founding member, but has refrained from withdrawing. When a China Airlines (CAL) cargo plane was forced to land in Guangzhou by a pilot who wished to defect to the PRC, the CAL representatives from Taiwan met with their counterparts from the PRC to negotiate a safe return to Taiwan of its crew, plane, and cargo. In 1987 Taiwan authorities bowed to suggestions made at home and abroad and began allowing Taiwan residents to return to the mainland to visit relatives.

Taiwan's Growing Economic Stature

A third major determinant of Taiwan's international role is its increased economic might. Taiwan has used its growing profile as a major international economic actor to quietly strengthen bilateral ties with the United States and with many Asian countries. For example, in 1979 the Taiwan authorities had only nine representative offices in the United States; in 1987 there were eleven. Taiwan and South Korea, long-time trade competitors, began to coordinate trade strategies, seeking to reduce their respective imports from Japan while increasing purchases from each other. And in Japan, as of 1986, roughly half of the Diet's Liberal Democratic Party members had joined the Association of the Japanese-Sino Parliamentarian Relations, a pro-Taiwan organization, a major increase from the earlier years. In addition, some of the opposition Democratic Socialist Party's Diet members formed a similar organization.

Taiwan's development experience is valued so highly by the member nations of the Association of Southeast Asian Nations (ASEAN) that quite a few dignitaries from these countries, which have no diplomatic relations with Taiwan, have visited Taipei (e.g., the vice-president and foreign minister of the Philippines and the minister of investment of Indonesia) in an attempt to encourage greater flows of capital and technology from Taiwan to their countries. In 1981 Sun Yun-suan, then premier of Taiwan, visited Indonesia and greatly expanded Taiwan's bilateral trade and investment relationship with that country. In 1984 Taiwan representatives in the Philippines, with which Taiwan enjoys no diplomatic relations, were granted diplomatic immunity. Ties with Singapore, Thailand, and Malaysia have also been strengthened. Malaysia's "Look East" policy (which emphasizes learning from newly industrializing countries like Taiwan) fits especially well with many Taiwanese businessmen's desire for joint ventures. Given Taiwan's currently large and growing foreign-exchange reserves, it seems highly likely that following the lifting of foreign-exchange controls and other liberalization steps, Taiwan will become an important exporter of capital as well as goods, thus further strengthening its economic ties with Asia.

Prospects

Despite such favorable trends, however, analysts remain sharply divided over whether Taiwan will continue to survive and develop as a viable international actor. As in the past, Taiwan's posture will be determined by the actions and balance of power among the major countries in Asia, the politics and policies of the PRC, Taiwan's economic and political stature in international affairs, and its continued stability in the wake of President Chiang's death.

In all likelihood, the power relations in Asia during the next decade, particularly Sino-Soviet relations, will be different and more complex than they have been in the recent past. For one thing, Soviet diplomacy will be far more active and imaginative. To be sure, Moscow will not—and cannot be expected to—abandon its acquired security interests in Asia (e.g., its base in Vietnam's Cam Ranh Bay). Nor will it pass up any opportunity to advance its interests at the expense of the United States, for example, by increasing its trade and diplomatic presence in the South Pacific, or at the expense of the PRC, for example, by selling more military equipment to and gaining more political influence in North Korea. But under Mikhail Gorbachev's leadership, the Soviet Union is likely to translate its new-found interest in Asia into concrete policies. Gorbachev has shown considerable skill in his dealings with Western Europe, and in his July 1986 speech in Vladivostok he showed a similar ability to reach out and touch the countries in the Western Pacific, appealing to the self-interest of those in each country. The Asia-Pacific countries, often neglected by Soviet diplomacy in the past, are now getting much more attention from senior Moscow officials. To the extent possible, Moscow will seek to supplement its military power with other policy instruments.

One should not be too surprised then if some or all of the "three obstacles" now claimed by Beijing to be existing in Sino-Soviet relations were to be removed one by one in the next fifteen years.[20] To the north, the riverine islands around the Chinese Northeast offer a good point for an initial breakthrough on the border issue. To the south, a political solution to the Vietnamese occupation of Cambodia, if accepted by the new leadership in Hanoi, is likely to be endorsed by Moscow, with obvious benefits attendant vis-à-vis the PRC and Southeast Asia. To the west, there is already less resistance in Moscow to a compromise over Afghanistan as witnessed by recent Soviet troop withdrawals in 1988. All of these possible developments will not change the fundamentally competitive relationship between the PRC and the Soviet Union, but should they materialize, repercussions will be felt throughout Asia. In particular, they could free PRC forces for possible use in areas of concern to Taiwan.

In contrast to the relatively optimistic outlook for Soviet policy in Asia, a number of developments may complicate Washington's future role in the region. The recently more assertive U.S. trade policy may clash increasingly with the development needs of the Asian countries. In particular, as Taiwan's trade surplus with the United States grows, it may come to be seen as a major cause of U.S. economic difficulty, and American support for Taiwan could decline. At a minimum, bilateral trade issues will continue to vex U.S.–Taiwan relations for the foreseeable future and will require able management on both sides in order to avoid serious crises detrimental to the bilateral relationship and, by extension, to Taiwan's security, stability, and prosperity.

Domestic troubles in two of Washington's key allies in the region, the Philippines and South Korea, will create painful policy dilemmas for U.S. policy as both countries struggle to make progress toward democratization. This process is complicated in the Philippines by a Communist insurgency and the need for dramatic economic reforms and in South Korea by the recent leadership transition and calls for increased liberalization. The United States may also face uncertainties growing out of the complexities of a possible Sino-Soviet rapprochement and internal PRC politics. These

[20] The obstacles refer to Chinese opposition to the Soviet military buildup along China's northern border, Soviet support for Vietnam's occupation of Cambodia, and the Soviet military occupation of Afghanistan.

changes and uncertainties in Asia, especially when taken together, may enlarge the range of debate within Washington's policy circles over the appropriate balance in U.S. policy toward the PRC and Taiwan. Under these circumstances, it is not inconceivable that a new U.S. administration would move to accommodate the PRC's demands at the expense of Taiwan, for fear of setting back important U.S.–PRC strategic, economic, or political relations.

As for the impact of the PRC's policy on Taiwan, several things appear firm. First, the PRC will not likely abandon its desire for reunification. After the Hong Kong and Macao agreements were signed, it seemed natural to PRC leaders to hope for an agreement on reunification of Taiwan. Second, if political trends in Taiwan and the mainland were to diverge further (e.g., Taiwan were to democratize and move toward self-determination and the PRC were to remain authoritarian), the ideological gap between them could widen markedly, with each pursuing the goals of modernization and growth by following widely divergent models. In the near and mid-term, this may create more pressure for Beijing to pursue an active policy toward Taiwan, pressing for greater contacts, trade, and interchange and working with third parties (e.g., the United States) to push Taiwan to be more open to PRC gestures. This could lead to a policy that is much more complicated, with uncertain implications for stability on the island.

In the past, the PRC's alternating practice of negotiating initiatives and making veiled threats to use force had been focused almost exclusively on the Nationalist leaders who came from the mainland in the 1940s. Increasingly, the PRC has been forced to appeal not only to these officials but to others who are also seen playing a key role in reunification policy. These include Taiwanese officials rising in the ranks of the Nationalist administration, opposition politicians in Taiwan, and American officials and opinion leaders, including a small but well-organized Taiwanese-American lobby in the United States. These individuals espouse divergent views as to how Taiwan's future status should be decided.

Since Taiwan's economic and, perhaps to some extent, political relations with other countries are likely to grow as its economy expands, Beijing may also attempt to tighten its pressure on Taiwan by isolating it diplomatically, particularly in Asia. As the economic gap in terms of per capita income between Taiwan and the mainland widens further, Taiwan may gain greater confidence in its international relations. To some extent, economic advancement may also help Taiwan build its defense base and strengthen its economic ties with other Asian countries.

Short of a direct provocation from Taipei (e.g., a declaration of independence, the establishment of relations with the Soviet Union, or production of nuclear weapons) or serious internal turmoil, it seems unlikely that the PRC would launch an invasion or institute a blockade against Taiwan. The main form of pressure would thus be diplomatic.

In this regard, the Republic of Korea (ROK, or South Korea) has been a prime target of Beijing's diplomatic efforts. South Korea is the only country in East Asia that still maintains diplomatic relations with Taiwan. But since 1973 South Korea has adopted a more flexible approach toward the Communist Democratic People's Republic of Korea (DPRK, or North Korea). Following a hijacking incident in 1983, the ROK began to have official contact with the PRC, and the volume and level of exchanges between the ROK and the PRC have greatly increased. In 1985 the two sides even started direct trade, and in 1988 ROK President Roh Tae Woo called publicly for improved relations with the PRC.

While this trend is worrisome to Taiwan, there appear to be distinct limits to the future relationship between the PRC and the ROK. As long as North Korea continues to insist on the principle of "one Korea," Beijing is unlikely to establish formal diplomatic relations with Seoul. Both China and Korea are divided nations. Up to this point, the PRC has held that just as there is only one China, which is represented by Beijing, so is there only one Korea, which is represented by Pyongyang. Should Beijing recognize the ROK under a "cross-recognition" or other scheme, it may successfully cause the diplomatic tie between Taiwan and the ROK to break, but it may also undermine its own "one China" policy. The existence of "two countries, two systems" in the Korean Peninsula could reduce the appeal of Beijing's "one country, two systems" formula for settling the Taiwan issue.

It would also be difficult for the PRC to downgrade further the existing relationship between Taiwan and Japan. There are currently no diplomatic relations between Taiwan and Japan, although there is extensive trade between the two (Japan enjoys a comfortable surplus in its trade with Taiwan), and the two share many strategic interests. Taiwan sits astride the sealanes important to Japan's commerce, and the two countries enjoy an active people-to-people relationship. There are few problems that may divide the two in the future. Even with greater Soviet involvement in the Pacific and a more fluid Sino-Soviet relationship, Japan is unlikely to cater to Beijing's wishes on Taiwan. In fact, there is reason to believe that a stronger and more assertive Japan would also seek to protect the status quo in the Taiwan Strait and would insist that the "China issue" be resolved peacefully.

Beijing could also be disappointed if it hopes to increase its influence and decrease Taiwan's role among the ASEAN countries, which have long been wary of their big neighbor to the north. Vietnam's occupation of Cambodia temporarily created a united front against Vietnam and its backer, the Soviet Union, and thereby led to attitudes more favorable to the PRC among the ASEAN member nations. But some, notably Indonesia and Malaysia, remain suspicious of Beijing's ultimate intentions. Should a political solution to the Cambodian problem be found, the glue that has bound them together could be weakened. Taiwan, on the other hand, poses no such threat to the ASEAN nations. Instead, it is a convenient source of capital and technology. While political necessity and the lure of the mainland market may justify for the ASEAN countries diplomatic ties with Beijing—it is conceivable that Singapore and Brunei may establish and Indonesia may restore diplomatic relations with the PRC—this will not be done at the expense of Taiwan. As long as Taiwan's economic and political experiences remain attractive, Taiwan will likely be considered by the ASEAN countries to be relevant to their own development.

Perhaps of more importance will be Taiwan's handling of the situation in Hong Kong as the colony reverts to PRC control. Hong Kong is one of Taiwan's most important trading partners: it is a valuable transportation hub for airlines and shipping lines operating to and from Taiwan; it provides ready access to information on developments in the PRC; and it serves as a forwarding point for mail and money from mainlanders in Taiwan to their relatives in the PRC, while remaining the most convenient place to arrange meetings with those relatives. It is also, along with Singapore, one of two Chinese societies outside the PRC with which the Chinese on Taiwan have developed a wide variety of interactions. The absorption of Hong Kong into the PRC, even under the rubric of "one country, two systems" agreed between the British and the PRC, means that after 1997 Taiwan must regard Hong Kong as part of the PRC. If Taiwan were to apply to Hong Kong the policies currently applied to the PRC, it would have to cut off direct trade and air, sea, mail, telegraph, and telephone connections. A wide range of other relationships between Taiwan and Hong Kong also would come to an end. For example, residents of Taiwan would only be able to visit Hong Kong under certain restrictions. Clearly, "PRC treatment" of Hong Kong after 1997 would be very costly to Taiwan.

From a practical standpoint, continuing to treat Hong Kong as an entity distinct from the PRC would have important advantages for Taiwan. The question is how such treatment could be rationalized and how its adverse effects on Taiwan's policy toward the PRC could be minimized. Taiwan has already begun easing its restrictions on contact with the mainland, while maintaining an official position against such contacts. During the coming ten years, further change is likely. At the same time, however, it is highly possible that the changes will not go so far as to bring Taiwan to accept fully the "three connections" involving communication, travel, and trade contacts advocated by the PRC, or eliminate all three of the "three no's" maintained by Taipei—no compromise, no contact, and no negotiation. Thus, in order to continue important contacts with Hong Kong while maintaining a credible policy vis-à-vis the mainland, Taiwan will probably have to come up with a policy for relations with Hong Kong after 1997 that eases the overall ban on contacts with the mainland and that treats the Hong Kong Special Administrative Region differently from the rest of the PRC.

In sum, Taiwan's position in East Asia at first glance appears precarious as it faces an insistent nuclear-armed neighbor determined to reassert sovereignty over the island. But closer examination shows that the interests of the regional powers are not served by substantial disruption of the status quo. And the Taiwan leaders have prudence sufficient enough to avoid actions (such as declaring independence) that would seriously undermine the regional status quo that has proven, on the whole, favorable to Taiwan's peace and prosperity.

VII. Conclusion

On balance, an assessment of key variables that will determine Taiwan's future strongly suggests that prospects for Taiwan's continued social, political, and economic development seem good. Barring unforeseen circumstances, Taiwan's international standing also seems secure. This is not to say that the authorities and populace on Taiwan do not confront numerous problems brought on both by the rapidly changing conditions on the island and by adverse international trends. Indeed, outside observers are correct to monitor closely the difficult leadership succession, the debate in Taiwan over greater political liberalization, and trends toward greater advocacy of self-determination by the Taiwan people, all of which could complicate the political stability that has prevailed on the island in recent years. Domestic economic and social trends appear less worrisome, although there remains a prevailing anxiety among Taiwan intellectuals and others about the future of the island and their role in it. In addition, economic planners remain unclear as to how Taiwan's family-centered economy will be able to generate resources sufficient to allow Taiwan to compete effectively with the developed economies in the international market.

Meanwhile, the main international danger appears to be economic rather than political or strategic. That is, trends toward protectionism in the United States and other major markets for Taiwan's exports could have a major effect on the island's prosperity and underlying sociopolitical stability. Nevertheless, the record shows that the people on Taiwan have been resourceful and shrewd in the past in protecting their interests in the face of worse challenges, and there is little evidence that they have lost their ability to position themselves well to deal with and adjust to change.

Economic, political, and social changes in Taiwan have added a series of important policy questions for Americans concerned with developments on the island. These come against a background of the continuing attempt by U.S. policymakers to establish and maintain a proper balance in the triangular U.S.–PRC–Taiwan relationship.

Economically, policymakers in the administration and Congress now are focused on Taiwan's successful export-oriented development and its large trade surplus with the United States. Specific questions include:

72

- What are the present and future competitive challenges to U.S. industries posed by Taiwan's economic success?

- Has that success been accomplished fairly, and what should the U.S. response to it be? Should we press Taiwan harder to open its markets to U.S. products? Should we restrict access to U.S. markets? Should we pressure Taiwan further to adjust the value of its currency and to restructure its economy?

- What opportunities are there for Taiwan investors to recycle their surplus funds back to the United States through investment here, and what would be the impact of such investment?

Americans concerned with the massive U.S. trade deficit call for strong action to improve the U.S. trade balance, possibly including limitations on foreign access to U.S. markets. They recognize that such action could negatively affect the economic prosperity and related political stability of a number of important U.S. trading partners, including Taiwan. But they judge that the United States has little choice but to take firm measures to protect its own markets and economic advancement.

A contrasting view comes from U.S. supporters of the Nationalist government, from Americans concerned with promoting greater political democracy amid continued economic prosperity in Taiwan, and from free-trade advocates who tend to oppose measures designed to restrict foreign exporters' access to U.S. markets. They emphasize the negative results for U.S. interests in Taiwan and for the international trading system that they believe would result from such restrictive trade legislation or administrative actions.

Politically, U.S. policymakers are called upon repeatedly to address issues related to the rise of a vocal political opposition movement in Taiwan. New issues will emerge as the leadership reorganizes in the wake of the passing of President Chiang Ching-kuo. Specific questions are:

- What role should the United States play in encouraging political liberalization in Taiwan? Is there a danger of serious instability if political change comes too quickly or too slowly?

- Which officials in the Kuomintang and the Democratic Progressive Party and which other opposition politicians seem most likely to follow policies agreeable to U.S. interests in the post--Chiang Ching-kuo period, and which, if any, would likely follow policies contrary to U.S. interests?

- Should the United States associate with DPP or other politicians who advocate political self-determination, which could possibly lead to independence for Taiwan?

Americans strongly concerned with promoting democracy abroad have joined with small but well-organized groups of Taiwanese-Americans to push for greater U.S. efforts to promote political liberalization in Taiwan. They argue that greater U.S. pressure is needed to force the Nationalists to reduce political restrictions and allow the development of a truly multi-party, democratic political system on Taiwan.

An opposing view comes from those Americans who identify closely with the Chinese Nationalist administration and urge U.S. support for the Nationalists' very gradual and incremental efforts to liberalize. Even among Americans who favor closer U.S. relations with the PRC, there are those who caution against U.S. support for liberal opponents of the KMT. They judge that liberalization might lead to a separate identity for Taiwan vis-à-vis the mainland, and they see such separation deepening the already serious U.S.–PRC differences over Taiwan. Ultimately this could lead to increased tensions in East Asia if China perceives a threat to its long-term goal of reunifying Taiwan with the mainland.

Internationally, current questions for U.S. policy in the U.S.–PRC–Taiwan triangular relationship center on:

- How far should the United States go in continuing the sale of arms or military technology to Taiwan? What are the circumstances that might justify a decline in U.S. sales?

- What should the attitude of the United States be toward efforts to establish for Taiwan a strong international identity distinct from the PRC, for example, as the "Republic of China" or as "Chinese Taipei"?

- What should U.S. policy be toward the advocacy of some elements in Taiwan for "self-determination," with its inherent risk of leading to a move toward independence from the mainland?

Such questions are likely to pose serious difficulties and dilemmas for U.S. policymakers well into the next decade. In particular, it is likely that none of them will be answered in isolation; these issues interact with and affect one another. American policymakers and opinion leaders will probably continue past practice and give

74

priority to specific interests rather than focus on these overarching questions of U.S. policy toward Taiwan.

Those in the United States who strongly support the Nationalist government (support that has been encouraged by that government's vigorous public relations efforts) will likely remain a well-organized and influential force in American politics. Generally, they judge that U.S. interests are best served by following policy options that support, or are compatible with, the concerns of the Nationalist administration. In particular, they encourage U.S. policy to take strong action to support Taiwan's international identity and security in the face of perceived threats from the Communist mainland. At present, they would like the United States to: back strongly Taipei's position vis-à-vis the PRC in international organizations such as the Asian Development Bank, using the Taipei administration's preferred title, the "Republic of China"; agree to high-level negotiations for a U.S.–Taiwan free-trade accord similar to those the United States has negotiated with other close allies, including Israel and Canada; supply Taiwan with more advanced weapons in larger quantities; and firmly rebuff PRC efforts to obtain U.S. support for contacts and negotiations between the PRC and Taiwan.

A contrasting set of policy choices comes from Americans concerned with developing closer economic, political, or military ties with the PRC. They stress that the United States should avoid actions with regard to Taiwan that they feel would provoke a negative response from the PRC. Thus, they support strict compliance with the U.S. commitment made in the August 17, 1982, U.S.–PRC communiqué to reduce arms sales to Taiwan. They also judge that the United States should not identify Taiwan as the "Republic of China" in the Asian Development Bank and other public fora. Some in this group also advocate U.S. support for PRC efforts to encourage contacts with Taiwan, even though the Taiwan administration may remain opposed to such contacts.

In the long run, the answers to all of these questions might well be determined largely by sociocultural developments. Will the younger generation of "mainlanders"—those who grew up and were educated on Taiwan and have less emotional attachment to the mainland—accelerate the process of integration into the native Taiwanese society, or will they remain a distinct elite? Will the power of the Chinese family as an economic unit weather the assault of modern Western influences, or will the dominance of family-centered, small and medium-size firms give way to dominance by a few corporate giants? Will Taiwanese society as a whole

75

drift further from its mainland roots, or will Taiwan draw closer to the mainland as trade and other contacts increase? As these issues are resolved over time, answers to questions about the probable course of change in Taiwan's political system, about its prospects for continued economic development, and about its international status will be made clear to those watching Taiwan enter the 21st century.

Appendix A
Conference Papers

Taiwan Entering the 21st Century
April 23–25, 1987
The Asia Society, New York, NY

"Taiwan's Winds of Change," Parris H. Chang, Department of Political Science, The Pennsylvania State University.

"The Question of Lifting Martial Law and the Enactment of the National Security Law in the Republic of China on Taiwan," Hung-dah Chiu, Professor of Law, University of Maryland School of Law.

"Taiwan's Relationship with Hong Kong," Ralph N. Clough, School of Advanced International Studies, The Johns Hopkins University.

"Taiwan's International Relations," Harvey J. Feldman, Consultant, New York, NY.

"Working Class Taiwan," Hill Gates, Department of Anthropology, Central Michigan University.

"Popular Culture and Society in Taiwan," Thomas B. Gold, University of California, Berkeley.

"The Middle Classes in Taiwan: Formation and Implications," Hsin-Huang Michael Hsiao, Institute of Ethnology, Academia Sinica, Taipei, and Department of Sociology, Duke University.

"Taiwan-Mainland Relations: The High Stakes of Risks and Opportunities," Michael Y.M. Kau, Brown University.

"Taiwan Entering the 21st Century—The Economic Challenge," Anthony Y.C. Koo, Michigan State University.

"The Chinese Tradition and Modernization in the Republic of China," Thomas A. Metzger, Department of History, University of California, San Diego.

"Taiwan Entering the 21st Century: The Economy," Ramon H. Myers, Senior Fellow and Curator-Scholar of the East Asian Collection, Hoover Institute on War, Revolution and Peace.

"Taiwan's Strategy for Creating Competitive Advantage: The Role of Foreign Technology," Denis Fred Simon, Sloan School of Management, Massachusetts Institute of Technology.

"The Republic of China and Asia," Chi Su, Institute of International Relations, National Chengchi University, Taiwan.

"Taiwan's Political System in Transition," Hung-mao Tien, University of Wisconsin.

"On the Role of Government in Taiwan's Industrialization," Robert Wade, Fellow, Institute of Development Studies, University of Sussex (based on his forthcoming book: *Guiding the Market: Taiwan's Industrial Policies in Comparative Perspective*).

"Economic Aspects of Political Liberalization on Taiwan," Edwin A. Winckler, Columbia University.

"Success and the Sense of Predicament: A Cultural Perspective on Modernization in the Republic of China," Thomas A. Metzger, Department of History, University of California, San Diego.

Appendix B
Conference Participants

Lili Armstrong
American Bureau for Medical
Advancement in China

Marshall M. Bouton
The Asia Society

Parris H. Chang
Pennsylvania State University

Hung-dah Chiu
University of Maryland

Y.S. Chow
The China Times Cultural
Foundation

Ralph N. Clough
School of Advanced
International Studies
The Johns Hopkins University

Patricia Farr
The Asia Society

John Fei
Yale University

Hill Gates
Central Michigan University

William Gleysteen
International Consultant
Former U.S. Ambassador to
Korea

Thomas B. Gold
University of California, Berkeley

Susan Greenhalgh
The Population Council

Harry Harding
Brookings Institution

Hsin-huang Michael Hsiao
Academia Sinica, Taipei
Duke University

James Hsiung
New York University

Chao-Sung Huang
The China Times Cultural
Foundation

Anthony J. Kane
The Asia Society

Michael Y.M. Kau
Brown University

Anthony Y.C. Koo
Michigan State University

William McCalpin
Rockefeller Brothers Fund

William McGrath
American International
Underwriters

Thomas A. Metzger
University of California,
San Diego

Douglas Murray
China Institute in America

Ramon H. Myers
Hoover Institution
Stanford University

Robert B. Oxnam
The Asia Society

Arthur Rosen
National Committee on
U.S.–China Relations

Denis Fred Simon
Massachusetts Institute of
Technology

Chi Su
Institute of International
Relations, Taiwan

Robert G. Sutter
Library of Congress

Hung-mao Tien
University of Wisconsin

Robert Wade
University of Sussex

Edwin A. Winckler
Columbia University

John Watt
Committee on International
Relations Studies with the PRC

Suggested Reading

Ahern, Emily Martin, and Hill Gates, eds., *The Anthropology of Taiwanese Society* (Stanford, CA: Stanford University Press, 1981).

Clough, Ralph N., *Island China* (Cambridge, MA: Harvard University Press, 1978).

Galenson, Walter, ed., *Economic Growth and Structural Change in Taiwan* (Ithaca, NY: Cornell University Press, 1979).

Gold, Thomas B., *State and Society in the Taiwan Miracle* (Armonk, NY: M.E. Sharpe, Inc., 1986).

Kuo, Shirley W.U., Gustav Ranis, and John C.H. Fei, *The Taiwan Success Story: Rapid Growth with Improved Distribution in the Republic of China, 1952–1979* (Boulder, CO: Westview Press, 1981).

Simon, Denis Fred, *Taiwan, Technology Transfer, and Transnationalism: The Political Management of Dependency* (Boulder, CO: Westview Press, 1988).

"Taiwan Briefing," *China Quarterly* 99 (September 1984). Includes articles by Susan Greenhalgh, Ramon H. Myers, Stuart E. Thompson, Byron S.J. Weng, and Edwin A. Winckler.

Tien, Hung-mao, *Political Dimensions in Taiwan: Continuity and Change in a Party State* (Washington, DC: Hoover Institute, forthcoming 1988).

Weng, Byron S.J., "Taiwan and Hong Kong, 1987: A Review," *China Briefing, 1988,* Anthony J. Kane, ed. (Boulder, CO: Westview Press, forthcoming 1988).

About the Author

Robert Sutter is Senior Specialist and Chief of the Foreign Affairs and National Defense Division of Congressional Research Service, Library of Congress. He received his Ph.D. in East Asian history at Harvard University. He teaches regularly at Georgetown University and University of Virginia; during 1988 he is teaching at The Johns Hopkins University School of Advanced International Studies.

Dr. Sutter is the author of several books on Chinese foreign affairs and U.S.–East Asian relations, including *Chinese Foreign Policy: Developments After Mao* (New York: Praeger, 1986).